W9-BQT-437

LESSONS FROM TEAM LEADERS

A Team Fitness Companion

Jane E. Henry, Ph.D.

ASQ Quality Press
Milwaukee, Wisconsin

Lessons from Team Leaders: A Team Fitness Companion
Jane E. Henry, Ph.D.

Library of Congress Cataloging-in-Publication Data
Henry, Jane E., 1934–
    Lessons from team leaders : a team fitness companion / Jane E.
Henry.
        p.   cm.
    Includes bibliographical references and index.
    ISBN 0-87389-382-4 (alk. paper)
    1. Teams in the workplace.   I. Title.
HD66.H458   1998   97-50123
    658.4′02—dc21   CIP

10 9 8 7 6 5 4 3 2 1

ISBN 0-87389-382-4

Acquisitions Editor: Roger Holloway
Project Editor: Jeanne W. Bohn

ASQ Mission: To facilitate continuous improvement and increase customer satisfaction by identifying, communicating, and promoting the use of quality principles, concepts, and technologies; and thereby be recognized throughout the world as the leading authority on, and champion for, quality.

Attention: Schools and Corporations
ASQ Quality Press books, audiotapes, videotapes, and software are available at quantity discounts with bulk purchases for business, educational, or instructional use. For information, please contact ASQ Quality Press at 800-248-1946, or write to ASQ Quality Press, P.O. Box 3005, Milwaukee, WI 53201-3005.

For a free copy of the ASQ Quality Press Publications Catalog, including ASQ membership information, call 800-248-1946, or access http://www.asq.org.

Printed in the United States of America

 Printed on acid-free paper

American Society for Quality

Quality Press
611 East Wisconsin Avenue
Milwaukee, Wisconsin 53202

Contents

Prologue ix
Acknowledgments xiii
Foreword xvii
Introduction: Why Teams? 1

A. Team Fitness: The Model 9
   Fitness Area 1: Customer Focus 10
   Fitness Area 2: Direction 13
   Fitness Area 3: Understanding 17
   Fitness Area 4: Accountability 19
   Summary 26

B. How to Use This Book 27

C. The Role of the Leader .31
   How Teams Are Formed .32
   Selection Of The New Team 32
   Poof! Suddenly, You're A Team! 35
   The New Leader In An Intact Group Or Team 36

Clean Up This Mess 37
Summary 38

D. Team Start-Up **41**
Launch the New Team with a Clear Charter 44
Prepare to Work Together 45

Start-Up Exercise No. 1—Customer Focus 51
**Customer Focus Interviews: One Department
to Another, Corporate to Field** 51
• Customer Focus Worksheet 54

Start-Up Exercise No. 2—Direction 56
New Team Charter 56
• New Team Charter Worksheet 58
• New Team Charter Summary Sheet 60

Start-Up Exercise No. 3—Direction 62
Charrette 62

Start-Up Exercise No. 4—Direction 65
Creating a Road Map 65
• Creating a Road Map Worksheet 68
• Creating a Road Map—Example 69

Start-Up Exercise No. 5—Direction 70
Building a Mission Statement 70
• Creating a Mission Statement Worksheet 73

Start-Up Exercise No. 6—Direction 74
Transition: Old Values to New Values 74

Start-Up Exercise No. 7—Direction 77
Creating a Vision with Words 77
• Creating a Vision with Words Worksheet 80

Start-Up Exercise No. 8—Understanding 81
Selection Interview 81
• Selection Interview Worksheet 83

Start-Up Exercise No. 9—Understanding 84
Getting to Know You 84
   • Getting to Know Your Team Interview Questions 86
   • Getting to Know You Worksheet 87

Start-Up Exercise No. 10—Accountability 89
Basic Principles 89
   • Basic Principles Worksheet 91
   • Basic Principles—Example .92

Start-Up Exercise No. 11—Accountability 93
Looking for Our Values 93
   • Start-up—Example 95

Start-Up Exercise No. 12—Accountability 96
Implementation Planning 96
   • Implementation Planning Worksheet 98
   • Critique of Implementation Plan Worksheet 99

Start-Up Exercise No. 13—Accountability 100
Meetings and Setting up the Rules 100
   • Meeting Rules Worksheet .102
   • Meeting Agenda—Example 104

Start-Up Exercise No. 14—Accountability 105
Team Values to Agreements 105

Continuous Improvement of Teams **107**
Introduction 107
Training 108
Cross-Training 109
Continuous Feedback 110
Two Major Frustrations 111

Continuous Improvement Exercise
No. 1—Customer Focus 117
The Voice of the Customer .117
   • Client Service Survey—Example 120

Continuous Improvement Exercise No. 2—Customer Focus . .122
What Will People Say? 122

Continuous Improvement Exercise No. 3—Direction 124
Creating a Vision with Pictures
What Is? What Should Be? 124

Continuous Improvement Exercise No. 4—Direction 126
Weighted Decision Analysis 126
• Weighted Decision Analysis Worksheet 128

Continuous Improvement Exercise No. 5—Direction 129
Bottled Lightning 129
• Problem or Process or Product
to be Studied Worksheet 131
• Bottled Lightning—Example 132

Continuous Improvement Exercise No. 6—Understanding . .133
Strategic 360° Feedback .133
• Peer Performance Review—Example 136

Continuous Improvement Exercise No. 7—Understanding . .137
360° Debrief 137
• 360° Debrief Worksheet 139

Continuous Improvement Exercise No. 8—Understanding . .140
Communication Networks 140
• Communication Networks Exercise 143

Continuous Improvement Exercise No. 9—Understanding . .144
Let's Read a Book 144
• Let's Read a Book Worksheet 146

Continuous Improvement Exercise
No. 10—Understanding 147
The Huddle 147

Continuous Improvement Exercise
No. 11—Understanding 149
If This Team Were a _ _ _ _ _ 149
• If This Team Were a _ _ _ _ _ Worksheet 151

Continuous Improvement Exercise
No. 12—Understanding 152
Alien Consultants 152

Continuous Improvement Exercise No. 13—Accountability .154
Look At All the Angles .154
• Look At All the Angles Worksheet 156

Continuous Improvement Exercise
No. 14—Accountability 157
Assault on Everest 157
• Assault on Everest Scenario 159
• Assault on Everest Worksheet 162

F. **Saying Good-Bye** **163**
Introduction 163
How to Disband the Team 164
Summary 165

Closure Exercise No. 1—Customer Focus 167
What Have We Accomplished? 167

Closure Exercise No. 2—Understanding 169
Peer Recognition Poster 169

Closure Exercise No. 3—Understanding 171
Prouds and Regrets 171

Closure Exercise No. 4—Accountability 173
How Did We Do? 173
• How Did We Do? Worksheet 175

G. **Celebrations** **177**

Epilogue 181

Bibliography 183

Index 185

Prologue

Dear Reader,

In my work with teams over the past 20-plus years, I have worked with companies to help them get organized, get back on track, or do whatever the needs of the group required. This experience has been very rewarding, and it has provided the basis for the first book I wrote with Meg Hartzler, *Team Fitness: A How-to Manual for Building a Winning Work Team.* One of the things I found during the experience of working with teams is that I always learned something new from the team or the team leader.

WHY THIS BOOK?

As a result of these experiences, I decided to write a book from the ground up, from the "grassroots." I did not set out to conduct scientific research. I wanted to find out what successful team leaders *really* did.

HOW THIS BOOK?

I began by asking nationally recognized consultants to give me referrals to successful team leaders so that I might interview them. I defined a team as a workgroup that does mutual decision making and has mutual accountability. I was looking for teams that worked together within large organizations or leading small businesses. As an aside, it is quite amazing how long it took these team building and organization development consultants to come up with the names of successful team leaders and how few they could recommend. I also knew some leaders with whom I had worked.

Additionally, I belong to two newsgroups on the Internet, and I asked those members for nominations and ideas for exercises. I received several of both from this effort. The group facilitation newsgroup has 600-plus members internationally and the teamnet newsgroup has about 1000 members internationally. The latter is a subgroup of ASQ.

I took it on faith that the people nominated were good team leaders and that they had successful teams. When the leaders were contacted, no one disputed the idea that he or she was a successful team leader.

I developed a series of questions:

1. What can you tell me about your team?

2. Why do you work as a team rather than as a manager and a workgroup?

3. How do you measure your success?

4. What are the frustrations, challenges, and problems you face in working this way?

5. What advice would you give to other team leaders?

WHO WERE THE TEAM LEADERS?

To find the answers to these questions, I interviewed more than 30 team leaders. These leaders came from various types of organizations: finance, health care, hightech, government, education, utilities, and small businesses. They led process teams, work teams, management teams, and cross-functional project teams. Some of them were supervisors, managers, and CEOs. Some leaders had no official power whatsoever.

My idea was to find out what worked for them—to understand the successes, and challenges, and frustrations they faced and how these leaders dealt with critical issues. Additionally, they gave me some processes and activities that would help other team leaders deal with their own teams.

The responses to these questions were sorted according to the Fitness Model (Hartzler and Henry, 1994, p. 3) under four categories: Customer Focus, Direction, Understanding, and Accountability. They were also sorted according to the main themes or trends that appeared in the data.

Most of the team leaders had little training in leading a team. They learned from reading, intuition, mistakes, and necessity. I do believe that each leader believes in the innate worth and dignity of every human being to operate as a team leader and be successful.

This belief allows team members to function at their highest capacity and display their own talents for work and learning.

This book is a synthesis of what I learned from these leaders, from reading others' work, and from personal knowledge and research. I have used the leaders' quotes liberally throughout. Occasionally, a name is with held upon the leader's request because of proprietary or personal reasons.

I am extremely grateful to the people who allowed me to interview them, those who nominated good team leaders, and those who contributed ideas for exercises. Their names are found in the acknowledgments section of this book.

MY VISION FOR THIS BOOK

It is my hope that this book will look like a good cookbook: that it will fall open easily to certain favored pages and be decorated with sticky notes and coffee stains. In other words, team leaders will *use* this book to help themselves become even more effective in their work. Furthermore, I hope that the stories and ideas from other team leaders will give you heart and new insights, particularly when you are stressed or blocked. I hope that I have communicated the fitness lessons from other team leaders to you.

I wish you the best success with your own team.

Acknowledgments

A book of this sort requires the efforts and expertise of a great variety of talents. I am extremely grateful to the following people who taught me new things and energized my writing.

Special thanks to the following team leaders who took the time to be interviewed by me and shared their expertise.

Anil Arora, *Vice President, Strategy and Marketing,* The Pillsbury Company, North America, Minneapolis, Minnesota

Gracie Coleman, *Vice President of Marketing and Corporate Support,* Lucent Technologies, Silver Spring, Maryland

Cheryl Cook, *State Director,* Pennsylvania Rural Development, U.S. Department of Agriculture (USDA), Harrisburg, Pennsylvania

Duncan Crundwell, *CEO,* Solid State Logic, Livonia, Michigan

Gary Dyer, *President/CEO,* FCS Southwest, Tempe, Arizona

Mary Fitch, *Deputy Director of Long Range Planning,* National Capital Planning Commission, Washington, D.C.

Jincy Fletcher, *Principal,* Flynn Elementary School, Westminister, Colorado

James Ford, *Director, Advocacy Training Center,* American Association of Retired Persons, Washington, D.C.

Bill Gardner, *Team Leader Organizational Development,* Advanced Micro Devices, Austin, Texas

Joan Gotti, *Vice President, Global Services Development,* Chase Manhattan Bank, Brooklyn, New York

Donna Hammond, *Senior Nuclear Specialist,* TU Electric, Glen Rose, Texas

Richard L. Herink, *Executive VP,* Supertel Hospitality Inc., Norfolk, Nebraska

Tyler Johnston, *Vice President of Marketing,* Dreyers Grand Ice Cream, Oakland, California

Judith Katz, *Senior Vice President,* Kaleel Jamison Group Inc., Washington, D.C.

Dean Lehman, *Core Team Leader,* Banc One, Columbus, Ohio

Richard McCool, *Manager of Health & Safety,* Gulf Power Company, Pensacola, Florida

Michael Milano, *President,* Murphy & Milano, Inc., Alexandria, Virginia

Bob Miller, *Vice President and Program Director of Information Technology,* Gates Rubber Co., Denver, Colorado

Jay Penick, *CEO,* Northwest Farm Credit Services, Spokane, Washington

Joseph L. Podolsky, *Manager, Planning & Quality for Corporate Information Systems,* Hewlett-Packard Corporation, Palo Alto, California

Nick Rakos, *Performance Specialist,* TU Electric, Glen Rose, Texas

Joel Reaser, *Director, Research and Technology,* American Association of Retired Persons, Washington, D.C.

Kurt Ronsen, *Human Resources Manager,* CoBank, Englewood, Colorado

George Schumaker, *Headmaster,* Green Hedges School, Vienna, Virginia

Jack Shuler, *CEO,* Pee Dee Farm Credit, Florence, South Carolina

Paula Siler, *Director of Professional Practice Affairs,* Harbor-UCLA Medical Center, Torrance, California

Al Thorbjornsen, *Director, Product Assurance,* Western Digital Corporation, San Jose, California

Terry Tierney, *President,* Allegro Coffee, Boulder, Colorado

Mike Turco, *Consultant,* Think Tank Consulting, Rancho Palos Verdes, California

Sunny Vanderbeck, *CEO,* Data Return, Arlington, Texas

Tracy Wagner, *Care Coordinator*, Menninger Clinic, Topeka, Kansas

Gerrold Walker, Vice President and General Manager, Sun Microsystems-Europe, Amsterdam, Netherlands

Emily Willey, *Director of Market Requirements & Government Relations*, Honeywell Inc., McLean, Virginia

Special thanks also to consultants and friends who recommended successful team leaders and provided ideas and input for exercises.

Members of TEAMNET, Internet LISTSERVE

Members of GROUP FACILITATORS, Internet LISTSERVE

Lynda Baker, *Lynda Baker Consulting*, Austin, Texas

Fran Coet, *Coet & Coet*, Westminister, Colorado

George Covino, *Babson College*, Babson Park, Massachussets

Pamela Dennis, *Destra Consulting Group*, Boulder, Colorado

Steve Dixon, *TU Electric*, Glen Rose, Texas

Vicky Farrow, *Lucent Technology*, Murray Hill, New Jersey

Jim Ford, *American Association of Retired Persons*, Washington, D.C.

Dell Gerstenberger, *Menninger Clinic*, Topeka, Kansas

Richard Gould, *Western Digital*, San Jose, California

Peter Grazier, *Team Building, Inc.*, Chadds Ford, Pennsylvania

David Hannegan, *Destra Consulting Group*, Boulder, Colorado

Roberta Harrison, *RJ Harrison*, Gulfport, Mississippi

Meg Hartzler, *Destra Consulting Group*, Boulder, Colorado

Bill Hefley, *Carnegie Mellon University*, Pittsburgh, Pennsylvania

Darcy Hitchcock, *AXIS Performance Advisors*, Battle Ground, Washington

Michael Hotz, *Farm Credit Council*, Denver, Colorado

Fiona Kidd, *Murphy & Milano*, Alexandria, Virginia

Ray Kramer, *Winter, Kramer, and Jessup, Architects*, Boulder, Colorado

Steve Merman, *SKM Associates*, Denver, Colorado

Michael Milano, *Murphy & Milano, Inc.*, Alexandria, Virginia

Theresa Noland, *Ranum School District*, Westminister, Colorado

John Post, *67th U.S. Intelligence Wing,* San Antonio, Texas

Pauline Russell, *Russell Consulting Group,* Boulder, Colorado

Charl Lee Sauer, *Ranum School District,* Westminister, Colorado

Roger Shaffer, *Farm Credit Council,* Denver, Colorado

Al Starkey, *Destra Consulting Group,* Boulder, Colorado

Terry Tierney, *Allegro Coffee,* Boulder, Colorado

Susan Tydings, *ST²Consulting,* Boulder, Colorado

Ed Webster, *International Mountaineer and Photojournalist,* Boulder, Colorado

Nancy Williams, *Murphy & Milano,* Alexandria, Virginia

Haz Wubben, *University of Colorado,* Boulder, Colorado

Then there are the people with whom I interact on a daily basis who need special thanks, the crew at Atkinson and Noland and Associates engineering firm, with whom I share office space and who provide encouragement and levity. My former co-author, Meg Hartzler, read, edited, and gave me encouragement when I needed it. Seneca Murley has been an invaluable person in layout and creativity and in helping me keep my act together. Peter Hesse, a talented illustrator, provided humorous and thoughtful drawings.

Thank you to the following Quality Press Reviewers for their helpful, insightful suggestions to improve the manuscript: Ronald L. Heilmann, Jill Phelps Kern, and Roy Richardson.

My dear husband, Jack Snider, the scientist, was my special editor. He had to learn to macro-edit, as well as micro-edit, and cook, too. Jack provided never-ending toleration of writer's block tantrums and gave enduring support.

Foreword

We are all on teams—if not in our professions then in our community lives. Even if we are not the titular leader of a team, we all influence the team's success by our effective participation.

Team leadership is a skill. For people to become good at any skill—whether it be athletics, music, or cooking—aptitude (talent), desire, coaching, and practice are required.

Aptitude is a limiting factor in many skills. Fortunately, however, there are few limitations to the skill of team leadership. The book you are holding, *Lessons from Team Leaders,* is designed to improve the skills of everyone on the team leadership path, whether they are novices or masters. This book provides a solid framework for looking into the key elements to a team's success. It gives the reader something to organize his or her own thoughts and experience around.

There are legions of team leaders who are looking for help to make their tasks a little more comfortable or at least less daunting. Jane has liberally included internal references and quotes from real practicing team leaders in a variety of settings from all levels of expertise. She brings us role models to show us what's possible, to increase our desire and confidence, and to motivate us to higher achievement.

Coaching, of course, is the main theme of this book. It is linked to Hartzler and Henry's first book, *Team Fitness: A How-to Manual for Building a Winning Work Team* (1994). If you are serious about mastering team leadership, you should read or reread that book; however, we can accomplish a lot simply by following effective methods and exercises. We can create great meals by following recipes, and we can create great teams by following the methods described here in *Lessons from Team Leaders*. Toward that end, I particularly recommend the tips from the pros that are sprinkled throughout this book as well as the many tools and templates that can be adapted to our own situations.

As many masters have observed, of course, of all the factors leading to great skill, practice is the most important—not just any practice, but practicing in ways that lead to continuous improvement. This book gives us the tools to implement effective team operations at all stages of the project life cycle, helping us to plan, measure, and learn and to achieve results.

As you probably already know, teams are not only inevitable but also fun. Grab the book, dive into your adventure, and enjoy.

Joe Podolsky
Manager, Planning and Quality Corporate Information Systems
Hewlett-Packard Company
Palo Alto, California
September 1997

Also available from ASQ Quality Press

Tools for Virtual Teams: A Team Fitness Companion
Jane E. Henry, Ph.D. and Meg Hartzler

Team Fitness: A How-To Manual for Building a Winning Work Team
Meg Hartzler and Jane E. Henry, Ph.D.

Mapping Work Processes
Dianne Galloway

Creativity, Innovation, and Quality
Paul E. Plsek

Quality Quotes
Hélio Gomes

Show Me: The Complete Guide to Storyboarding and Problem Solving
Harry I. Forsha

Show Me: Storyboard Workbook and Template
Harry I. Forsha

The Change Agents' Handbook: A Survival Guide for Quality Improvement Champions
David W. Hutton

Understanding and Applying Value-Added Assessment: Eliminating Business Process Waste
William E. Trischler

Value Leadership: Winning Competitive Advantage in the Information Age
Michael C. Harris

LearnerFirst™ *Process Management* Software
with Tennessee Associates International

To request a complimentary catalog of ASQ Quality Press publications, call 800-248-1946.

Introduction: Why Teams?

The pace of organizational change, the global challenge from the competition, the

> *I t's like breathing air. I don't know any other way to work.*
> Joe Podolsky, Hewlett-Packard

need for speed and expertise—these factors all lead to working in teams. If you are not a member of some team, you will be. These teams are found primarily in the workplace but also in not-for-profit boards, the local PTA, your city government, state and federal government, education, and health care. The team is an increasingly common phenomenon of the twenty-first century.

■ 1. Tasks are too complex for one person to do alone.

We need to bring many diverse talents and expertise to projects. Things are changing too fast for any one person to know all that needs to be known about a project or topic. Team members also know more different programs and technologies than any one person can know.

> *Too much is coming too fast from too many directions. There are so many moving parts, customers, variables. We're going where no one's ever been before.*
>
> Sunny Vanderbeck, Data Return

> *We needed to get where we wanted to go in a short period of time and I couldn't do it alone.*
>
> Richard McCool, Gulf Power Company

> *It's the only way to work. This job is too important and too complex for one person. It has to reflect the different facets of American life. I can't imagine doing it any other way.*
>
> Name withheld upon request

> *We also have to model teamwork and diversity in our own consulting work. The work is too complex for any one person. Each person brings different competencies to the table.*
>
> Judith H. Katz, Kaleel Jamison Consulting Group, Inc.

> *To survive, we have to work as teams. We have to rely on the expertise we have in order to do more with less.*
>
> Paula Siler, Harbor-UCLA Medical Center

■ 2. Teamwork leads to better decisions and results.

Companies that operate internationally need a global perspective to prevent miscalculations and mistakes at product introduction. Teams are less likely to miss things. The implications of various actions are found better through the use of teams because of the opportunity to get different perspectives.

Many team leaders credit teamwork for their financial success. One CEO said that his company was essentially bankrupt three years ago. But through teamwork and continuous improvement, they pulled themselves out of a deep hole and now do 50% more business with 25% fewer people.

T eams get the product out the front door faster, cheaper, and products are not returned for rework through the back door.
Al Thorbjornsen, Western Digital

W e wanted a pristine implementation for customers, sales force, management, and employees. This was the only way we could get it, through teamwork.
Dean Lehman, BancOne

S ince we started working in teams, we have replaced all products, increased productivity by 29%, and doubled sales volume.
Name withheld upon request

I 'm results-oriented and you get better results from teams—that's why I prefer to work with teams. Bring together the best talents, understand that give and take is crucial, then develop capability, ability. In a team you feed off each other's strengths—sort of like self nourishment for the team.
Donna Hammond, TU Electric

3. Teamwork stimulates innovation and creativity.

Problems, projects, and issues require many diverse points of view. The team or department can't become an island working in a vacuum. Innovation and new ideas are crucial. A diverse team provides lots of eyes and ears, giving different perspectives and points of view. Working in teams means that the reality of the new ideas can be more easily determined.

Teams can blossom with new ideas, innovation.

*I*f we didn't use teamwork, then I'm the only one thinking.
> Jack Shuler, Pee Dee Farm Credit

*W*e can use each other as backboards and improve our shots. Everyone has different altitudes from which they survey a problem, from the ground level to the eagle's point of view.
> Tyler Johnston, Dreyer's Grand Ice Cream

*W*hen I was with Mattel Toys, we had cross-functional teams to create new toys. There were engineers, marketing, design, manufacturing. We had to move the toy from design idea through safety to manufacturability, to market with continued quality improvement, cost reduction, and without recall. It took all of us to do it.
> Mike Turco, Think Tank Consulting

*W*hen I came to the new job, people were begging to become a team. We did things in six weeks that would have normally taken six months.
> Name withheld upon request

■ 4. Improved communication and buy-in and ownership of decisions results from teamwork.

Communication is better with everyone involved. The leader doesn't have to sell the decision in the end because it's been hashed out at each step of the process.

Through working as a team, people can understand the big picture and strategies, and everyone can participate in decision making. This results in mutual accountability as well as sharing in the rewards of a successful project. Planning and delivering a new product, process, or way of doing business gives everyone the incentive to make it happen.

*W*e owned the team together and held each other accountable for results.

Gracie Coleman, Lucent Technologies

*I*f you don't care who gets the credit, it's amazing what can get accomplished.

Jack Shuler, Pee Dee Farm Credit

5. Teams can create a more enjoyable work climate where everyone has the opportunity to succeed.

Through teamwork, everyone can have a feeling of achievement, as well as the freedom to do things, to innovate. In the manager and workgroup relationship, people's abilities are often under-utilized. Teams make it possible to use each person's abilities and talents to the fullest.

Employers and employees buy into teamwork in part because it's more fun than the old manager-workgroup situation. One leader reported introducing teamwork to a long-established workgroup. The longtime employees were at first suspicious, but once people broke free and found they could do things differently, they became creative, energized. Now they had the opportunity to fix things that they knew were wrong.

*T*eams are connective, human, energizing, evocative, everything that direction is not.

Name withheld upon request

People feel needed, wanted. Work is a joy. It's fulfilling.

> *O*ver and above our products and services, one of the greatest successes of the team was the commitment and sense of satisfaction of the members of the team. Within a conservative organization, with strong traditions, we created a fluid, level, opportunistic, multidisciplinary, and effective team.
>
> Joel Reaser, AARP

> *I* like working with successful people. We learn from each other. The better they get, the better I get. I enjoy watching each person's individual growth. Each of them could go into another organization and run it.
>
> Jay Penick, Northwest Farm Credit Services

> *I*t was tough getting started working as a team, but now we do things automatically. We throw problems on the table, look for the root cause and decide what to do. We've had no turnover. People have had opportunities for promotions, but they turned them down. "I've never had so much fun in my life," they say. It's never boring.
>
> Richard McCool, Gulf Power Company

> *I* like the idea of self-managed teams. I have enjoyed seeing the team grow as a team, functioning at levels they couldn't do before. I like the open communications. I like to see the people grow, acquire new skills, become comfortable to take chances.
>
> Tracy Wagner, Menninger Clinic

6. Successful team leaders prefer to work this way.

Team leaders prefer to share decision making by involving the people who are affected by the decisions. They don't believe in giving orders as the way to get things done. Rather, they attempt to obtain the maximum effectiveness from each team member's special talents and abilities.

> *A*s a team leader, I don't like to dominate. I like to be in on things, but be able to use the resources of those in the organization and the community.
>
> Jincy Fletcher, Flynn Elementary School

By their nature, most of these team leaders prefer a collaborative style. They are more comfortable sharing the decisions, jointly solving the problems in innovative and creative ways, and sharing the rewards of a job well done.

> *When you empower the team, the pace picks up. Who's driving the bus? It's not linear. You're not in control. You look, review, accept, go. You have to learn to play by a new set of rules.*
> Nick Rakos, TU Electric

> *Just do it. No matter what the frustrations, it makes the leader's job easier.*
> Michael Milano, Murphy & Milano, Inc.

So, Why Teams?

Tasks are becoming so complex that we need a diversity of expertise to compete in the marketplace. Working in teams can stimulate innovation and creativity leading to superior decisions and results. Teamwork enhances communication and mutual accountability and can lead to a climate where everyone has the opportunity to work to her full potential. Successful team leaders prefer the excitement that often comes from teamwork.

A. Team Fitness: The Model

Team leaders and managers who find themselves in the position of building a new team or revitalizing an existing one appreciate having guidelines and checklists to use.

In our previous book, *Team Fitness: A How-To Manual for Building a Winning Work Team,* Meg Hartzler and I developed a model for teams to follow to become more effective. This chapter briefly describes the model and shows you where team leaders reinforced the model, deviated from the model, or carried the areas forward.

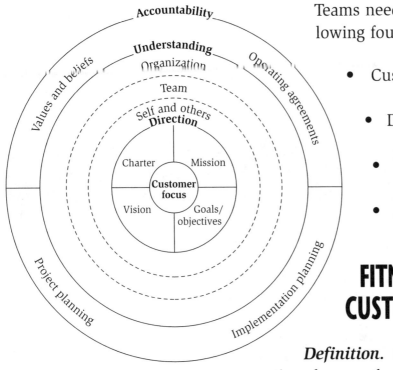

Figure 1. Team fitness.

Teams need to concentrate in the following four areas:

- Customer focus

- Direction

- Understanding

- Accountability

FITNESS AREA 1: CUSTOMER FOCUS

Definition. *Customer focus* means getting clear on the expectations, values, and priorities of those who receive your work and ensuring that those expectations shape the requirements for the products and services your team provides.

Factors. Customer focus has two parts: *identification of customers* and *clarification of the customers' requirements and expectations.*

What Did The Team Leaders Say?

Successful team leaders are well aware of their customers. They know who the customer is and what the customer wants and needs. Systems are in place to define customer expectations and track performance against those expectations.

Customers may be internal people or departments or the entire organization. Some customers are the final, ultimate buyer of the products and services (for example, a consumer, a student or parent, or a patient in a hospital). Sometimes the customer is a supplier.

Project teams are often formed to solve problems in the break-down between internal suppliers and customers.

> *O* *ur team and the plant were out-of-synch with each other. Their problems needed to be solved within 36 hours. Our processes were elaborate, with lots of analysis and talking. Sometimes the problem would die on the table, being talked to death. By that time, the people in the plant would have solved the problem and moved on. In order to splice the disconnect between the team and the plant, we went to the customer. First of all we moved into proximity with the customer. Next, we decided to find out what the customer expected from us. How did we do it? We simply went to the customer and asked. Armed with the customer service requirements, the team members sat together and problem-solved and prioritized the customer needs and how best they could meet them. They set a standard of a 24-hour turnaround time for all customer requests.*
> Name withheld upon request

Another company formed a team to bring itself into compliance with more than 125 regulatory standards. The team worked together to determine current performance, graphed it on a bar chart, and monitored compliance. In less than two years, the company had met compliance at 95% of standard. The goal for the team is to reach 100% compliance by February 1, 2000.

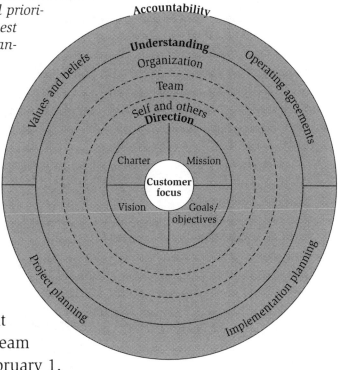

Figure 2. The first fitness area—customer focus.

The customer is seen as a partner. Together the teams solved problems. This theme also carried through to the internal and the external customer or the supplier.

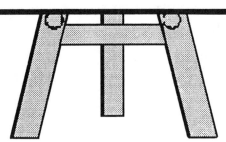

Client Interview Questions—Example

1. Tell me what led you to call me? (You're going to hear it all anyway. It's best to let this catharsis take place early so you can move on.)

2. What should be happening that isn't?

3. If we define the problem in this way, have we defined all the problems?

4. How will you know when the problem is fixed?

5. How does everyone else see or feel about this problem?

6. How long do we have to fix this?

7. Where will the funds to fix this problem come from?

8. If we change these behaviors with this result, will you consider the project successfully completed?

FITNESS AREA 2: DIRECTION

Definition. <u>Direction</u> defines the unique contribution of the team, from its broadest purposes to its specific actions and activities. Direction shows the fit between the team's purpose and the organization's purpose.

Factors. Direction is composed of the following four factors:

1. *Charter*—Formally putting the team into existence

2. *Vision*—Creating a mental image of what you want your team to contribute in the future

3. *Mission*—Defining your purpose and your unique contribution to the enterprise

4. *Goals and objectives*—Broad statements of the desired end results with objectives that spell out the specific actions and activities to obtain those results

What Did The Team Leaders Say?

Most team leaders had invested the time to plan up front and to build their vision, mission, and major goals and objectives. Goals and objectives had quantitative measures of some kind. Large charts often marked progress against goals and milestones.

*E*stablish your goals. Define your success. What is victory?
Donna Hammond, TU Electric

*I*t takes longer to get them to see the vision. Once you get buy-in, implementation is shorter.
Cheryl Cook, Pennsylvania Rural Development, USDA

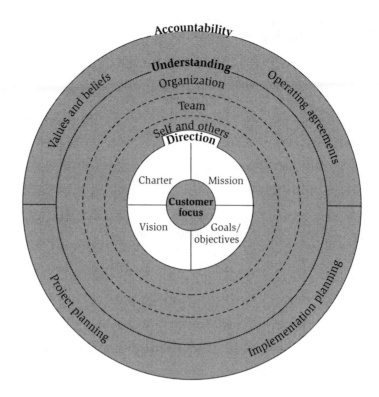

Figure 3. The second fitness area—direction.

Mission Statement—Example

*D*ata Return provides interactive Websites to companies who are serious about doing business on the Net.

Sunny Vanderbeck, Data Return

Mission Statement—Example

*O*ur product is a researcher who is methodologically and technologically up-to-date.

Joel Reaser, AARP

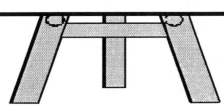

Mission Statement—Example

Green Hedges school is committed to providing a classical education to a socially and culturally diverse group of children.

Believing that happy, relaxed students learn best, we provide a safe, intimate environment and caring teachers.

We inspire each child to master academic skills, to develop clear values, to experience joy, and to appreciate all human endeavors which broaden the mind and enlighten the spirit.

Green Hedges School

Profitability and team contribution to profitability were well-tracked. Several teams taught everyone how to read the financial reports and how to track their shares in the profitability of the company.

J ob security comes from profitability. We believe in open book management and that means training every employee to understand your business.
Rich Herink, Supertel Hospitality Inc.

Some teams were divisions of larger, hierarchical companies. Teams in those organizations can look vague or haphazard; however, when they deliver on results and/or generate more profit, they are allowed to continue to operate as a team.

Many internal teams had sponsors who helped set the direction, build the charter, and break down barriers. One team had a formally signed charter that served as a contract between the company, the sponsor, and the team.

> *M*ake sure you're clear on what you want. If you're the sponsor, spend good, quality time on what you want the team to accomplish.
>
> Gerrold Walker, Sun Microsystems

> *I*n order to deliver results, we must use the technical and human expertise at our command. The temptation is to spend 98% of our time on the technical. We must pay attention to the human side. Even with the best intentions, it takes great concentration of energies to pay attention to the human side.
>
> Bob Miller, Gates Rubber Company

Small businesses often begin with the senior management team's strategic plan. This plan is translated into the team unit's plan, which becomes one of contribution and commitment by the individual.

One leader moved from one team to another. She said that the new team was foundering. When asked "Why?" she explained that the goals and the purpose of the new team were too vague.

In general, BHAG's (Big, Hairy, Audacious Goals, from Collins and Porras, 1995, p. 94) were the norm. If anything, it seems that one of the main problems with teams is that people are so energized that they commit to more than they can physically do.

FITNESS AREA 3: UNDERSTANDING

Definition. <u>Understanding</u> means learning and interpreting the inherent nature of ourselves, our team members, and our organization.

Factors. Understanding is composed of the following three factors:

1. *Self and others*

2. *Teams*

3. *Organization*

What Did The Team Leaders Say?

Balance was a major theme in most of the interviews with team leaders. They were concerned about the balance between members' personal lives and growth, the team's work, and providing service to the larger organization or the customer.

The chapter Team Start-Up, the section on team member selection and development, explains more about the team leader's role.

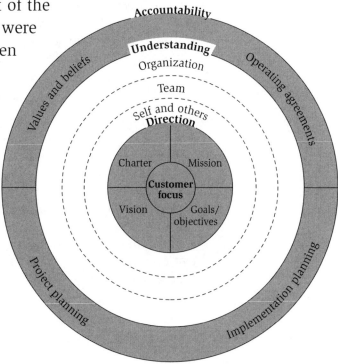

Figure 4. The third fitness area—understanding.

O *urs is a global team. That way we can work on problems around the clock. We also travel a lot to various sites. At the same time, we try not to interfere with people's personal lives. We strive to balance work and personal life.*

Joe Podolsky, Hewlett Packard Company

Special concern with physical space was a surprise finding.

W *e knocked all the walls down. Now sales personnel and engineers all sit together. It increased communication, increased spirit. Now we all see that everyone's working hard and see what everyone is doing. Everyone answers the phone. The receptionist became the sales coordinator.*

Duncan Crundwell, Solid State Logic

Creative teams and "pressure cooker" teams had freewheeling outlets for energizing team members. Some teams used nerf frisbies, bells to ring when a small victory was scored, pinball machines, table tennis, kids' toys, and Disney wallpaper.

D *on't get frustrated or give up. When you hit a difficult spot, sit down and hash it out. Often it has to do with paradigms and you need to help the paradigms shift. We have different beliefs and philosophy. Get it resolved and then all will feel better.*

Al Thorbjornsen, Western Digital

I *know intellectually that not everyone is like me. Not everyone wants a challenge. Reward for me may be punishment to them.*

Donna Hammond, TU Electric

T *o provide team members with a better understanding of the business, Allegro sent a large group of the team leaders to Guatemala to see the coffee growing and meet the farmers. You can't believe the heightened excitement and passion for quality that they now display.*

Terry Tierney, Allegro Coffee

Teams meet regularly to share results and learning.

> *O*ur team was formed during a time of down-sizing. People wanted the truth. We would meet three times per week and talk. I would tell them, "This is rumor. This is fact."
>
> Nick Rakos, TU Electric

The leader often acts as a liaison to the rest of the organization.

> *I* see my role as clearing the path for them, to work with the executive council, upward communication, remove barriers, take care of outside complaints, and act as a buffer. At the same time, I watch the development of each individual, push people to try new things, and provide a safe environment.
>
> Richard McCool, Gulf Power Company

FITNESS AREA 4: ACCOUNTABILITY

Definition. Accountability is the willingness to be responsible for the results the team is expected to achieve, specific projects and plans, and to be responsible to one another.

Factors. The following four factors influence the team's accountability:

1. *Values and beliefs*—The beliefs, held by the organization and the team, by which the team is expected to live

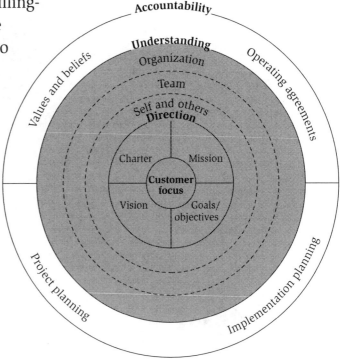

Figure 5. The fourth fitness area—accountability.

Being accountable for others is tough.

2. *Operating agreements*—The ways team members agree to behave and work together

3. *Project planning*—The planning methods used to ensure that the right things are done and that they are done right, in the right sequence, and on schedule

4. *Implementation planning*—The planning methods used to ensure that the project plans and the work of the team will be accepted by the rest of the organization

What Did The Team Leaders Say?

The four factors of accountability received a great deal of attention from the team leaders. The team leaders were pragmatic and idealistic at the same time. They believed in the use of basic values to drive their team and build operating agreements. These agreements were seen as essential to preventing conflict and misunderstanding in reaching the team's objectives.

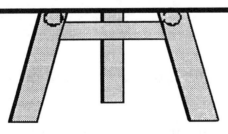

Core Values—Example

We are a company that cares about people and their health.

Each of us is a leader as well as a team player in our campus community.

Community means caring, belonging, trusting, and sharing pride in our achievements.

All members of our community choose to be active learners, listeners and innovators.

Recognition and commitment to excellence are values we cherish.

Energy is focused on patient care, education, and research.

Together we create a community of quality patient care, quality work life and an effective organization.

Harbor-UCLA Medical Center

We made mistakes around our core values. We had too many. And not every one of the values was a make or break value. Now we've narrowed them to three. These are values that we will not give up, even with changes in the environment.

Jack Shuler, Pee Dee Farm Credit

*W*ork together up-front to develop guiding principles. Some of ours are:

1. Leave your stripes at the door,

2. Respect everyone,

3. Look for different points of view,

4. Start on time; end on time,

5. Everyone has input into the agenda, prior to their walking in the door.

Joan Gotti, Chase Manhattan

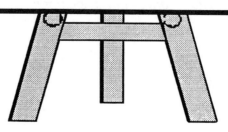

Ground Rules—Example

RELIABILITY MANAGEMENT
CONTINUOUS PROCESS IMPROVEMENT TEAM

1. All meetings will start/end on time and members will return from breaks on time.

2. Meeting minutes will be alphabetically rotated among all members and the leader. They will be published within 2 working days of the meeting and will contain old/new business as well as an agenda for the next meeting.

3. Movement within the room by all members is allowed.

4. The team will conduct business under the guideline of mutual respect.

5. Everyone will participate in the meetings.

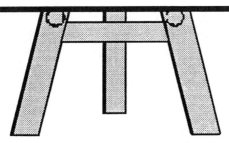

6. Every voice gets heard.

7. Only 1 person speaks at a time.

8. Members will give the team advance notice in the event of absences.

9. Meeting locations will be flexible.

10. Members will copy secretaries on changes to travel.

11. Meetings will convene with a quorum of 2/3. This is 4 persons minimum.

12. The team will conduct meetings under the confidentiality rule.

13. If the leader is missing, a back up leader will be a team member.

14. Ground rules can be amended.

Al Thorbjornsen, Western Digital

Most teams developed methods for confronting one another, and peer pressure was the most frequent technique used. Sometimes team leaders had to confront missed deadlines and a failure to live up to agreements. They didn't like to do it, but they believed it was necessary.

H old people accountable on day-to-day commitments and deadlines. Even if you don't like to do it, confront people honestly
and quickly. Give feedback. Deal with issues directly.

Gary Dyer, Southwestern Farm Credit Services

—◆◆◆◆◆—

R ely on peer pressure to deal with member's failure to live up to
expectations and deadlines.

Al Thorbjornsen, Western Digital

Because many of the teams were internal, their major product
or success was measured in terms of whether their ideas were
implemented by the rest of the organization. Therefore, they spent
a great deal of time up front and throughout the team's life planning for the project and its implementation.

Stakeholders were prominent in their thinking. Input from, and
communication of progress to those concerned with the team's
output were well planned, not thrown over a wall in the hopes
that someone would catch it.

H old people as able to perform and hold them accountable.

Gracie Coleman, Lucent Technologies

—◆◆◆◆◆—

W e send 'flash messages' to stakeholders. We tell them about
the new or improved process, its status, and where we are on
the project.

Al Thorbjornsen, Western Digital Corporation

—◆◆◆◆◆—

W e use communication to keep the rest of the organization
informed about our progress. We make regular announce-
ments in the company paper and hold town meetings to gather
input and answer questions.

Bob Miller, Gates Rubber Company

Summary

The team leaders we interviewed used all parts of the Team Fitness Model, which is meant to be used at any place in the life of
the team. Team leaders see the process more sequentially, so this
book is organized accordingly. The exercises make reference to the
Team Fitness Model.

B. How to Use This Book

Lessons from Team Leaders: A Team Fitness Companion is meant to be a how-to manual with specific emphasis on the sequential phases of the team's evolution. We begin with the Role of the Leader and the Start-up Phase, then move to Continuous Improvement and Dissolution. Each exercise is labeled according to the Team Fitness Model and the stage of the team's life. You will need to assess your own situation and your own team and then pick the tools and techniques that fit best for you. The choices you make and the sequence you use will vary according to the time your team will be together and where you begin in terms of trust, success, and relationships. Over time, your team can take a step-by-step approach to diagnosing its needs and planning for and carrying out team activities.

Team leaders see the formation and development of teams in a linear fashion. Invariably, they begin with the **start-up** and move through the maturation of the team with emphasis on **continuous improvement.** Inevitably, most teams **dissolve** as the mission changes, people move on, or a project is completed. Suggested activities, tools, and advice are given here under each of these cycle headings.

Consider the stage your team is in. Are you in the start-up phase, or are you or maturing into continuous improvement? Look at the exercises and view the four elements at each phase of the team. Each exercise has an identified purpose and suggestion on "when to use." Choose the exercises that fit your team's needs.

Note: Leaders of established teams are encouraged to look over the exercises in the start-up section of this book. There may be areas there where your team can benefit by revisiting some sections or fill in portions of overlooked activities.

The following matrix can be used to determine quickly the appropriate exercises to be used at each phase of a team's development. The matrix lists the phases in the life cycle of a team in the rows and the four fitness areas in the columns.

TEAM EXERCISES BY FOCUS AND PHASE

	Customer Focus	Direction	Understanding	Accountability
Start-Up	Customer Focus Interviews: One Department to Another Corporate to Field	New Team Charter Charrette Creating a Road Map Building a Mission Transition: Old Values to New Creating a Vision with Words	Selection Interview Getting to Know You	Basic Principles Looking for Our Values Implementation Planning Meetings and Setting Up the Rules Team Values to Agreements
Continuous Improvement	The Voice of the Customer What Will People Say?	Creating a Vision What Is? What Should Be? Weighted Decision Analysis Bottled Lightning	Strategic 360° Feedback 360° Debrief Communication Networks Let's Read a Book The Huddle If This Team Were a _ _ _ _ _ Alien Consultants	Look At All the Angles Assault on Everest
Saying Good-Bye	What Have We Accomplished?		Peer Recognition Poster Prouds and Regrets	How Did We Do?

C. The Role of the Leader

This section of the book begins with the role of the leader at different phases in the life of the team. The leader has to decide when to be directive and when to be supportive. The leader's role is impacted by how the team is formed. Blanchard's Situational Leadership Model (1990), applied to teams, makes an appropriate framework in which to consider the leader's role. Simply put, the amount of direction and support provided by the leader is related to the team's competence and commitment and the different phases in the life of the team.

> *A t first my role as team leader was to deal with upper management. Later, the team came to me with a problem. I offered to go to plant management with them. I knew they were a mature team when they said, "We're just telling you. You don't need to go with us."*
> Nick Rakos, TU Electric

How Teams Are Formed

A team start-up can result from different scenarios.

1. It may truly be a brand new team that is formed to become a new department, to work on a project, or to solve a problem. In this case, the leader begins with a new slate of members.

2. It may be an intact work team or business unit, and the leader is the manager. The company decides that this group will become a team, or the leader may decide that he wants to change management style to work more as a team. In these cases, the problem is learning your new roles.

3. The team may be an intact workgroup that gets a new leader who wants to work as a team. This case requires direction and support.

4. A team is in place but it is not functioning well, and a new leader is assigned. More directive skills are required here.

Selection Of The New Team

New teams begin every day. Leaders who are lucky get to choose the members of their teams. This situation is often the easiest of all for any team leader. Leaders are most careful in how they select team members. You will need the special talents and resources for the job; at the same time, you'll want people who are not like you.

Criteria for selection to the team is one area where everyone agreed. ***Choose diversity.***

Bring together diverse talents and expertise.

- Choose people with different skills.

- Choose people with different perspectives.

- Look for passion and potential. Some people who don't do well in a hierarchical or "lone-ranger" environment blossom in a team environment.

*W*e were in a downsizing mode. I had to turn down people who were unskilled, and those who would be put at risk by leaving the department. Then some people just didn't want to team.

Nick Rakos, TU Electric

1. *Hire (select) tough.*

2. *Look for different backgrounds, diversity. If they have the same skill set, choose the one who is more different from others in the team.*

3. *Walk the thin line between individual and group rewards. Balance the two.*

4. *Constantly doubt what you know about teaming. Teams change and are dynamic. Reexamine your assumptions.*

5. *Be humble. Continually strive to do it better. Stay attuned and open to feedback.*

Bill Gardner, Advanced Micro Devices

*H*ire smart people. Frame out the architecture. Take a first cut at where we're going. Put them close to the issues and stay out of the way. But make them work together to reach consensus.

Tyler Johnston, Dreyer's Grand Ice Cream

1. *Don't pick people who are like you.*

2. *Pick people you can trust.*

3. *Pick people who see things differently and will challenge you and the group.*

Cheryl Cook, Pennsylvania Rural Development, USDA

*P*rovide balance. If I could design a team from scratch, I'd look for the strength in differences. Not everyone is first out of the block. Optimize what people bring to the team. Synergy vs. Superstars. I'll take synergy every day.

Gerrold Walker, Sun Microsystems

*W*e are currently working on our hiring criteria. Who works best in this environment? We have agreed that we will not hire super-stars. We're looking for team players.

Jack Shuler, Pee Dee Farm Credit

I met with everyone separately and then together. I asked them, "What are your hopes, your expectations, your concerns of being on this team? What do you want out of taking this risk to join this team? What are you shooting for? I'll help." Sometimes it was advancement, exposure, changing job skills. I committed to do everything I could to meet those needs and then I did it.

Nick Rakos, TU Electric

Poof! Suddenly, You're A Team!

There are times when you, as the manager of a workgroup, suddenly become a team leader. You're supposed to operate differently and share decision making and accountability. This may be an uncomfortable situation for you and your team members.

*W*e did extensive cross-training to get everyone up to speed in every area. It was frightening and overwhelming. Some thought it was impossible, ridiculous. We were persistent. We worked on definitions—common understanding of what to do and how to do it. We became a team that can do everything efficiently. It's never boring. The team members were surprised at themselves. They like the empowerment, at being able to decide what to do and then do it. My co-workers kept looking over their shoulders after making a decision, wondering if it were really true. Was I going to take the decision back?

Tracy Wagner, Menninger Clinic

B *e honest with the team and with yourself. You have a new job title. You're no longer a supervisor. You run up against something and then you find yourself making the decision and not involving the team. Step back and think again.*

Nick Rakos, TU Electric

Y *ou have a supervisor role and yet we must work together to perform at a higher level as a group than we could individually.*

Jay Penick, Northwest Farm Credit Services

W *ait for team members to ask for help; don't take decisions away from them.*

Duncan Crundwell, Solid State Logic

The New Leader In An Intact Group Or Team

It can be very difficult for the leader to step into an existing work-group, especially if the group has been together for some time. Some members are going to want to continue doing "business as usual." They will want to continue to work their piece of the pie. They are not at all interested in sharing decisions and accountability. They are not interested in operating this way. An intact team can be terribly set in its ways. One suggestion to change the prevailing team culture was to change the composition of the team by adding new members.

As a leader, you must first get to know each team member.

- Who are they?

- What skills and experiences do they bring to the table?

- What are their aspirations for themselves and the team?

- If they were in your shoes, what would they do?

> *W*hen the team was reformed, I met with each person at his
> site. I asked them to tell me:
>
> - *What is your role?*
> - *What do you do?*
> - *What goes right?*
> - *What gives you heartburn?*
>
> Dean Lehman, BancOne

> *K*eep things in perspective; remember it's not a life and death
> matter.
>
> Donna Hammond, TU Electric

> *M*y role is to interface with outside stakeholders to ensure that
> recommendations are followed. It is boundary-spanning,
> weaving in and out of different organizations to achieve the goals of
> the benefits plan. We marshal various vendors and consultants, rec-
> ognize that we do some things well, others not so well and it's bet-
> ter to out-source.
>
> Kurt Ronsen, CoBank

In contrast, another leader who inherited a group of long-term, set-in-their-ways employees found them to become absolutely energized by the idea that they could define their vision and mission. Once they realized the truth that they really could make a difference and redefine their roles, they set out to correct the faults of the system where they worked.

Clean Up This Mess

Another way to inherit an intact work team is to be brought in to clean up a situation that is not working. The team has been together for some time, and suddenly here comes the new leader. They will test you, just like a child tests a new step-parent.

Several leaders that I interviewed described the above experience. Two people began by setting up new ground rules.

*N*o more missed deadlines. The deadline does not move. Up until then, people didn't feel obligated to deliver. People would come to explain why they couldn't meet a deadline. The deadline does not move. I had to discipline myself against pressure to move the deadline. Now people are coming forward with analysis, problem-solving. Now they help each other. How can I help you get back on schedule?

Bob Miller, Gates Rubber Company

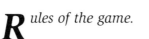

*R*ules of the game.

1. *Proactive communication. When you get new information, stop and think: "Who else needs to know?" Information stops with you and people have to find out somewhere else. That is not acceptable.*

2. *Share all deliverables with others. Input might slow you down, but make sure everyone sees, reads, hears.*

3. *We are going to make mistakes. How will we deal with it?*

   - *Fix the problem*

   - *Fix the process*

   - *DO NOT fix the blame*

Dean Lehman, BancOne

Summary

Leaders advise, **Patience.** Wait and see. Some members will retire from the fray. They'll quit or move to another part of the organization. Others may need to be helped out or replaced. One leader found that nonplayers became a support staff for the rest of the team. Another leader found that nonplayers acted as a balance to the energy of the team.

*T*he leader is the coach, the facilitator. We set parameters. The team makes the decisions.

Paula Siler, Harbor-UCLA Medical Center

*H*ave patience. It's good to have visions and share them and wait for the buy-in. At the same time, I need to be more directional. I want everyone to succeed, but sometimes I give them too much rope. You need a balance between the two.

George Schumacher, Green Hedges School

Most leaders have more experience in leading teams than the members of the team do in being on a team. The leaders see themselves as getting the team up and running and providing a safe environment for people to empower themselves. In the beginning they will be more directive, but later they see themselves more in a coaching or supportive role.

I told them. Look, it's like you're freshmen. We all have to learn this together. But we'll move on. By the time we graduate, you'll be seniors.

Gerrold Walker, Sun Microsystems

*W*e have a unique concept here. They're used to "spoke management." I need to pull out of the center.

Richard McCool, Gulf Power Company

*G*et in the way on the front end. Protect them early on. Then be willing to move out of the way.

Gerrold Walker, Sun Microsystems

Many leaders have led several teams and know that it is a scary undertaking for many team members. Other members are excited at the prospect of working independently and working together.

> *I encourage people to make decisions. They were surprised. Often people are looking for the leader to make all of the decisions. The operation is too big, too complex for one person. Team members limit themselves because they can't redefine their own job and work through to growth. They want to manage tasks as if they have to do everything themselves, just as they had in the past.*
>
> Rich Herink, Supertel Hospitality, Inc.

For experienced leaders, a big frustration is **time:** the time it takes for a team to gel, the time it takes for team members to trust one another and the process, and the time it takes to make decisions.

> *I have treated them like responsible adults and they have become responsible. It's a slow process.*
>
> Duncan Crundwell, Solid State Logic

> *Team leadership is a mantle of authority which floats among the people on the team.*
>
> Donna Hammond, TU Electric

> *It all comes back to this:*
>
> - *Hire the best people*
> - *Pay at the high end of the range*
> - *Take care of them*
> - *Recognize them*
>
> *Lay out where you want to go and hire people who want to go there.*
>
> Gary Dyer, Southwestern Farm Credit Services

D. Team Start-Up

New team start-up is very exciting and somewhat overwhelming. It seems that everything needs to be done at once.

First, you have to select your team or get to know the one you've inherited. You need to define the customer and their needs. You need to get clear on direction, build your vision and a mission, and set goals and objectives. You need to understand one another, what each person brings to the table, and how best to use your strengths. You need to define your values and build your operating agreements. Then you have to plan the project, set some milestones, and plan for implementation. Whew!

There is hope. That's the purpose of this book—to help you chart the way.

*D*on't be afraid to invest time up front. Develop the team and train them in change competencies. If you don't, it's a killer.

Bob Miller, Gates Rubber Company

---

*Y*ou must invest time and effort up front. This investment will pay off in the best team.

Anil Arora, The Pillsbury Company

If you're the CEO of your own company and you are starting a new team or revitalizing your existing one, you will probably begin with the business plan.

Jay Penick, CEO of Northwest Farm Credit Services, described the steps this way.

Develop a vision, mission, core values.

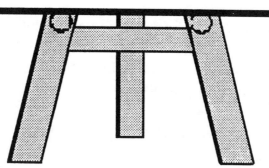

Philosophy of Business Plan—Example

Organizations annually review the prior year's progress and look to the future, revising or implementing processes and procedures as required to reaffirm a commitment to accomplishing the mission of the organization, and to insure that its mission, as stated in the past, is applicable to the future. This is the process of developing a business plan. There are three major drivers of a successful business plan as set forth below.

The Mission Statement—The organization's public statement of goal and purpose. The image of the organization as viewed by the customer and competitor is formed by successful accomplishment of this statement.

The Vision Statement—The organization's internal statement setting forth the areas to which the organization must be committed if it is to be successful in achieving its mission.

The Core Business Values—A statement of the organization's operating culture or environment, and the components which make up that culture. Through communication, training, and staffing, the business philosophy is instilled throughout the organization, putting in place the commitment necessary to accomplish the Vision Statement which in turn enables achievement of the Mission Statement.

Northwest Farm Credit Services

Start-up is a critical factor in the success of the team and its ability to work together in a self-directed way. Frequently, teams will come together and immediately begin the work without getting clear on their *charter,* the scope of the work, and how they will work together.

If you and your team will take the time up front to get clear on these two issues, you can save yourselves endless hours of floundering and of frustration at not being productive.

Launch the New Team with a Clear Charter

The charter should clarify the scope of the team's work, the expectations for the team's output, and the business need for this new team.

The charter should answer each of the following questions:

1. What processes or products is this team responsible for? Why are they important to the organization?

2. What boundaries or requirements are fixed?

3. Who is the chartering agent or sponsor? Who reports to that person?

4. What authority and decision-making power does the team have?

5. Who needs to be informed and when?

6. What are the team's deliverables? Are there milestones or time lines in place?

7. Who will measure the team? How will the team be measured?

Prepare to Work Together

If you have time and money, take the team off-site to do this start-up work. If not, find the time to get the team launched properly. How much time is enough? It depends on how much experience the team has had together, how long the team will work together, and the importance of the team's work.

▬ 1. Get to know each other.

Even if members know one another, they need to get to know one another in the context of this team. This enables everyone to know the strengths, work and communication styles, and the background and experience each member brings to the table.

> *I started out to change the culture of the team, break the mold.*
>
> *1. We changed the dress code. We were working outdoors in Florida. Everyone wears 100% cotton, no ties, no heels.*
>
> *2. No time cards. We don't work 8–5. We come and leave and get the job done.*
>
> *3. We came together often in the first several weeks. We outlined the areas for improvement and the opportunities.*
>
> *4. We made sure that we all shared the same perceptions.*
>
> Rich McCool, Gulf Power Company

> *We took the time up front to form the team.*
>
> Anil Arora, The Pillsbury Company

> *There is a learning curve on how to work together and get to know each other.*
>
> Kurt Ronsen, COBank

▄▄ 2. Focus on the customer.

Identify the team's customers and what you think those customers want and need. (A customer is defined as the recipient of the team's work.) Customers can be internal or external. The team might also have numerous customers, end users, or interim users. Determine the primary and secondary customers of the team.

> *W*e can be more responsive to customer requirements as a team. We provide specialized, custom-design solutions. Every job is different.
>
> Duncan Crundwell, Solid State Logic

▄▄ 3. Develop ways to track customer satisfaction.

Ascertain the wants and needs of the primary customers and the methods for measuring their satisfaction now and in the future so that results can be tracked.

▄▄ 4. Develop a vision and/or a mission for the team.

Time spent here will help the team clarify its reason for being and its unique contribution to the organization.

> *W*e had choices of where we wanted to go. We defined our vision and mission and used it over and over during the course of the three year life of the team.
>
> Anil Arora, The Pillsbury Company

> *W*e invested time up-front to go away and ponder. We arrived at a mission, a vision, and a strategy. We looked at where the business is going and how our roles fit in. Now we stay focused on a critical few objectives.
>
> Gracie Coleman, Lucent Technologies

▄▄ 5. Set the team's goals and objectives.

Consider the team's charter, customers, and mission. Build goals and supporting objectives to accomplish the work of the team.

B *e clear in your expectations. Be clear about the deliverables. Be clear about the use of the team members' time. Don't meet to meet. Set a fast pace to completion.*

Emily Willey, Honeywell Inc.

W *e have a commitment to the plant. We will answer their questions within 24 hours. Everyone has beepers. Our home phone numbers are published and they can call us there.*

Nick Rakos, TU Electric

I *f you don't do the up-front work, you will pay the price in the long run with poor work, frustrations, and floundering.*

Judith H. Katz, Kaleel Jamison Consulting Group, Inc.

6. Sign up for accountability to the goals and objectives.

Who does what around here? And who helps them? Clarify roles and responsibilities to prevent conflict resulting from overlap or things falling through the cracks. Clarify who is accountable to whom and for what.

B *ring them in and get clear on the objectives and the expectations. Learn about each other and how best to use each person's style and skills.*

Judith H. Katz, Kaleel Jamison Consulting Group, Inc.

7. Build a set of operating agreements.

These agreements will spell out how the team will work together. They should include agreements around meetings, delivering bad news, decision making, deadlines, and whatever has the potential to lead to conflict.

W *e have ground rules. In decisions on spending, the rule is to decide as if it were your own money. We can't allow the customer to suffer because of no decision.*

Duncan Crundwell, Solid State Logic

*W*e developed a set of team norms. We made a commitment to discuss concerns. It was our responsibility to solve problems together. We also decided we were going to have fun.

Nick Rakos, TU Electric

---

*A*t the initial meeting, develop a set of ground rules.

Al Thorbjornsen, Western Digital

---

*W*ork together up-front to develop guiding principles.

Joan Gotti, Chase Manhattan Bank

---

*W*e stressed four basic principles

1. Speed to market

2. Focus on the customer

3. Quality of product

4. Establishing a culture where it is comfortable to challenge each other.

Anil Arora, The Pillsbury Company

▧ 8. Build a tentative implementation plan.

At this stage in the group's work, this might not be possible on a definite basis. However, this is the time to begin planning for over-coming barriers, for communicating with key supporters, and for getting necessary resources.

▧ 9. Discuss rewards, recognition, and celebrations.

Create ideas for celebration of milestones, depending on how long the team will be together. The leader might want to meet with each member separately to understand how that person likes to be rewarded, recognized, and feel valued.

*D*evelop a recognition system. We have monthly department meetings. We use lots of thank you notes. We have "Thank you" packs to make it easy for everyone to say thanks when some-one does a service for them. We also have a Recognition Award Cab-

inet with lots of items on it under $20. People can go to the cabinet, leave a note on the board about the person who has done them a service and give one of the gifts to the person who helped them.

Bob Miller, Gates Rubber Company

Build a safe environment where it's OK to make mistakes, to challenge, and to grow.

I'd like to build a chain link fence around them so they could do their work without other distractions. A chain link fence so we can see what's happening in the rest of the organization and they could see how we work.

Rich McCool, Gulf Power Company

———⟨≋≋≋≋⟩———

1. *Value the nature of teams.*

2. *Respect each individual's perspective.*

3. *Nurture the team along.*

4. *Hold the team to their agreed upon outcomes.*

5. *Do fun activities for recognition and reward to build morale.*

6. *Create cross-functional networks.*

7. *Use heterogeneous groups. People can get things done when they know the other people and solve problems faster.*

8. *For team development, be persistent and tenacious. Let them know you care.*

9. *"Proceed until apprehended."*

Paula Siler, Harbor-UCLA Medical Center

———⟨≋≋≋≋⟩———

1. *There's no one style of leadership that works. You have to make a realistic assessment of the situation and decide when to be directive, when to be supportive.*

2. *Make sure you establish a vision and a mission, one that is exciting and inspirational.*

3. *Invest time and energy and work with people to build trust and credibility.*

4. *It's a process of constant learning. Situations arise that cause one to nudge and push. Leadership is both an art and a science.*

Anil Arora, The Pillsbury Company

Customer Focus Interviews: One Department to Another, Corporate to Field

Workout Plan

When to use

To identify expectations between the head or corporate office and field offices or between departments that must work together. This exercise can also be used between a senior management team and lower levels of management. It can also be adapted to use with external customers.

Time

Face-to-face: at least 2 hours; one-on-one: 1/2 hour per interview. 1 hour for debrief and planning.

Materials

Customer Focus Worksheet
Flip chart and markers for debrief

Purpose/Objectives

- To clarify the expectations among different parts of the organization

- To prevent miscommunication and conflict

- To help each group function together more effectively

Grouping

Appropriate members of various teams that interact with one another

Warm-up

Some groups in corporate headquarters believe that organizational members who work in the field are their customers. To define the expectations of these field customers, they bring in representatives to a central location and conduct a focus group session on the Customer Focus Worksheet. If face-to-face groups aren't feasible, the questions can be asked one-on-one and the responses tallied.

Aerobics

1. Choose the questions you want to ask the field personnel. Use the Customer Focus Worksheet as a guide.

2. Agree on the most effective method for getting the information (e.g., group, face-to-face, outside party, questionnaire).

3. Determine the ground rules for using the information.

   Examples

   - Confidentiality

   - No recriminations

   - Agree to do something with the information

   - Report to all members who participated

4. Gather information through questions.

5. Bring together all data and summarize at team meeting.

6. Debrief

- What do we like that we heard?

- What surprised us?

- What isn't clear? Does anyone have an example?

- What things will we agree to that we will not/cannot change?

- What suggestions will we change/act on?

- What would we like from them?

7. Develop a plan for disseminating the information and agreements to all participants.

Note: This process can also be used as a two-way communication tool through which the field offices ask the same questions of corporate headquarters.

Cooldown
Agree on a follow-up plan to see how new ideas are implemented and how well received they have been.

Adapted from ideas by Cheryl Cook

CUSTOMER FOCUS WORKSHEET

Here are suggestions for interviewers. This format may be used one-on-one, but is preferable with a group of four to six members of the internal customer group. There should be two people from the corporate or interviewing group: one to question and one to write notes. As you write notes, try to capture the exact words and phrases of the people being interviewed without stopping the flow of dialogue.

For the interviewer, this is a time to listen. The perceptions of the customer (field) group may be different from your own perceptions, but don't explain or try to change those perceptions. Simply listen and record.

Be sure to thank them for their time and information. Let them know they have been heard and that you will use the information they have given you to improve your products and service to them.

Questions

1. Tell us about what you do and how you see your primary mission.

2. Tell us about specific things that we do that help you in your job.

3. How do you perceive what we do in the home office or group?

4. What other things could we do that would be useful?

5. What are specific things that we do that hinder your performances?

6. If we could change just one thing, what would it be?

7. Overall, how would you rate our performance with you?

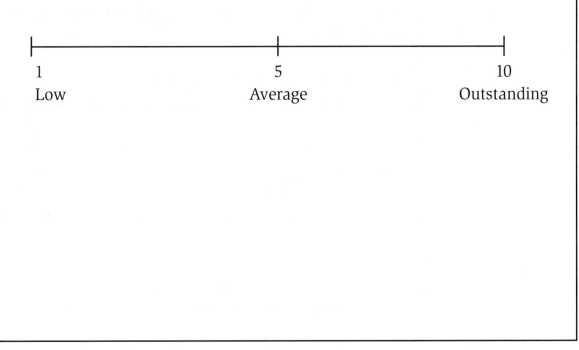

1	5	10
Low	Average	Outstanding

New Team Charter

Workout Plan

When to use
At the first meeting of a new special team or project team.

Time
30 to 60 minutes

Materials
Agenda made from the New Team Charter Worksheet and the New Team Charter Summary Worksheet

Purpose/Objectives

- To start up the first project team meeting with clear, structured information

- To make certain that basic team expectations and the scope of responsibilities are clear and shared by all team members

- To proactively answer questions that help create a context for teamwork

- To provide opportunity for team members to clarify areas of uncertainty

Grouping
All project team members and sponsor

Warm-up

Welcome all team members. Plan a short activity to help team members get to know one another better.

- If members have not met, have them share information about themselves that others need to know.

- If members know one another, share one thing that others would be unlikely to know, such as a memory from before the age of 10.

- In all cases, have everyone share their ideas on why they were chosen to be on this team.

Aerobics

1. Give general project information if needed.

2. Introduce the sponsor, if there is one. (This person needs the chartering questions in advance to prepare thoughtful comments.) The main agenda belongs to the sponsor or leader. Move through the agenda in an interactive way.

3. Provide a question-and-answer time for questions of any kind about the project.

Cooldown

After the sponsor finishes the agenda, he or she is free to leave. The team leader debriefs by summarizing and agreeing on the key points made and recording them for future use on the New Team Charter Summary Sheet. The team may wish to move on to other fitness exercises.

Note: The sponsor is the person who puts the team into being, to whom the team is accountable, and who is officially responsible for the team.

NEW TEAM CHARTER WORKSHEET

Key Topics for Agenda

Overview of project scope and definition

- Underlying purpose of the project

- Scope and expected outcomes

- Key processes for which team is responsible

Why the project is important to the organization

Why the project is important to team members (the business case)

Why each team member was selected for the project

Background information/situation explanation

Customer information/requirements/needs

Team expectations

- Autonomy/authority

- Who and when to consult/inform

- Expected deliverables

- Time line

- Resources

- Boundaries/restraints

- How the team will be measured

NEW TEAM CHARTER SUMMARY SHEET

Team: _____

Date: _____

Sponsor: _____

1. Key processes for which the team is responsible

   • _____

   • _____

   • _____

   • _____

   • _____

2. Expected deliverables or work output

   • _____

   • _____

   • _____

   • _____

   • _____

3. Key measures of team's work

- _____

- _____

- _____

- _____

- _____

4. Expectations for how to work (e.g., givens, boundaries, and considerations)

- _____

- _____

- _____

- _____

- _____

Charrette

Workout Plan

When to use
At the beginning of a new project, where you obtain input from many diverse points of view. When you want to build ownership in a product, process, or project by those people who will be involved in the implementation or use of the output of the team.

Time
1 to 2 hours

Materials
Flip charts and markers

Purpose/Objectives

- To build common ground on a particular problem or project

- To get many points of view on the table in a short period of time

- To blast through extraneous matters to the heart of the issue

- To bring multiple talents together to provide design guidelines

- To build common goals quickly

Grouping

Representatives of stakeholder groups who will be involved in the project's implementation or will use the output(s) of the team. All members of the team if the project stays within the team.

Warm-up

Charrette is a French word that describes a certain kind of cart used in the late 1880s. Historically, it was used to carry art and architecture students from their own studios to the Ecole des Beaux Arts. The charrette would come around and pick up the students. It is said that often the students, as usual, would be working on their projects in the charrette, frantically trying to finish them before their arrival at the school.

Currently, the word is used to describe a quick process used by architects and public planners to get ideas on the needs of the stakeholders and to record divergent points of view so they can be incorporated in the final design.

Aerobics

1. Define the problem or project that is facing the group.

2. Ask each person to think quickly about the obvious things that need to be incorporated into the project—those things that would make or break it for that professional person or that stakeholder group. No supporting rationale or data are required.

3. After all the requirements are listed on the flip chart, ask the group if anything is missing, if anything can be combined, or if anything can be eliminated.

4. At this point, the design team may thank the stakeholders for their input and begin to work on the project with the promise of reporting back to the group.

    OR

5. If the group is full of professionals with diverse talents, you may break the project into smaller pieces, let different groups work on the design, and meet at the end of the day and share solutions.

Cooldown

Thank the stakeholders for their participation. Explain that we have now built common ground for the project. The work today is a framework, a sketch, but it contains the basic elements of the final product.

Adapted from ideas by Ray Kramer

Creating a Road Map

Workout Plan

When to use

When the team is forming or at any point when things change. When you want to build a tangible illustration of the products or processes of the team. This helps the team to see how each member's part fits into the whole. Quality teams will recognize this as a continuous improvement process map.

Time

2 hours or more (unless the team is well versed in building a project plan)

Materials

Any designated process map or template that is in use in the organization

A copy of the team's charter and deliverables with deadlines

Flip chart, markers, and sticky notes

Creating a Road Map Worksheet

Purpose/Objectives

- To build a road map for the team's project

- To gain clarity around the sequence of efforts and how they fit together

- To think through the different steps in the process

Grouping

All team members

Warm-up

Hand out the Creating a Road Map Worksheet before the meeting. Ask members to think about the steps involved in the project.

Ask members to try to envision the points and the major milestones along the way from the beginning to the end of the project.

Aerobics

1. Brainstorm the various steps in the project.

2. Arrange sequentially.

3. List these steps horizontally across the top of flip chart paper.

4. Mark milestones and major completion points.

5. Ask members to write actions (on sticky notes) that are required at each point in the project.

6. Stick the notes under the steps.

7. Combine ideas and eliminate duplications.

8. Get consensus that these activities are necessary and sufficient to accomplish the step.

9. If possible at this time, put some deadline dates at each significant milestone.

10. Determine what measures are or should be in place to know that the team has hit its goal.

11. After the map is completed, ask members if they feel it is correct. Is it realistic?

Cooldown

After the map is completed and typed, set a time to revisit it to look for unnecessary steps or holes in the plan. When the plan is completed and agreed on, make sure everyone has a copy. Then make a large chart that everyone can see and check off the activities and steps as they are completed.

Note: Later, you will want to study your plan and decide who will do what and who will work with whom. Also, will you need to import outside resources for different activities?

Adapted from ideas by Al Thorbjornsen

See
Example
Page

CREATING A ROAD MAP WORKSHEET

Make notes on what you believe are the major steps in the project and the

activities you think fall under each step to accomplish it.

**Where We Are
What's in Place**   Step 1   Step 2   Step 3   Step 4

-
-
-
-
-
-

CREATING A ROAD MAP—EXAMPLE

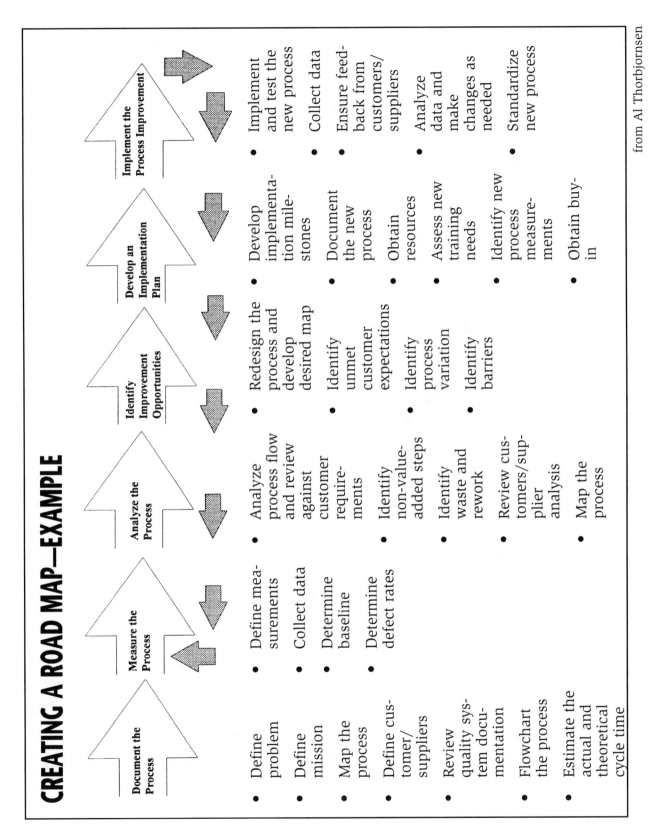

Document the Process
- Define problem
- Define mission
- Map the process
- Define customer/suppliers
- Review quality system documentation
- Flowchart the process
- Estimate the actual and theoretical cycle time

Measure the Process
- Define measurements
- Collect data
- Determine baseline
- Determine defect rates

Analyze the Process
- Analyze process flow and review against customer requirements
- Identify non-value-added steps
- Identify waste and rework
- Review customers/supplier analysis
- Map the process

Identify Improvement Opportunities
- Redesign the process and develop desired map
- Identify unmet customer expectations
- Identify process variation
- Identify barriers

Develop an Implementation Plan
- Develop implementation milestones
- Document the new process
- Obtain resources
- Assess new training needs
- Identify new process measurements
- Obtain buy-in

Implement the Process Improvement
- Implement and test the new process
- Collect data
- Ensure feedback from customers/suppliers
- Analyze data and make changes as needed
- Standardize new process

from Al Thorbjornsen

Building a Mission Statement

Workout Plan

When to use
When the team is starting up or at any time when the purpose of the team needs to be clarified.

Time
1 to 2 hours

Materials
Flip charts and markers
Building a Mission Statement Worksheet

Purpose/Objectives

- To define the purpose of the team

- To provide a baseline for decision making among priorities

- To gain agreement on the mission and purpose of the team

Grouping
All team members

Warm-up
Pass out the Building a Mission Statement Worksheet ahead of time and ask members to think about the questions on it. Explain that the purpose of a mission statement is to tell the world why

you exist. A second purpose is to guide your own thinking on making choices among various options.

Aerobics

1. Post four flip charts on the wall.
    Label them: "Activities We Do"
    "Activities We Could Do"
    "Activities We Will Not Do"
    "Activities We Can't Do"

2. Each person walks around the room and writes comments under each label.

3. When everyone is finished, read from each sheet of paper. Look for the themes, areas of agreement, and areas of disagreement.

Note: The activities that you do or could do help point your direction; activities that you will not do or can't do provide refinement.

Now define your mission.

We _____ (team name)	
exist to provide _____ (what?)	
for whom _____	
why? _____	
Any other qualifiers? _____	

4. Get consensus that this is the mission of your team.

5. Test the mission statement by hypothetical requests for services from others and through possible opportunities for new products, service, profit.

6. Wordsmith your statement to gain the greatest clarity and maybe a little pizzazz.

Cooldown

Decide how you want to use your mission statement. Where do you want to put it? Who else needs to see it? Discuss how this exercise may have clarified each person's thinking about the purpose of the team.

CREATING A MISSION STATEMENT WORKSHEET

To create the mission statement, consider the following:

- Who is our customer?

- What products and services do we provide?

- What do we provide for the customer that is unique?

- Why does the customer need us?

At the end of this exercise we should have developed one statement that expresses the collective thoughts of the group.

_____ exists

(organization)

to do what? _____

for whom? _____

why? _____

Transition: Old Values to New Values

Workout Plan

When to use

When a team is assigned to a new leader, when team members are shuffled and a new team is formed, when the mission of the team has changed, or when the company has reorganized or merged

Time

1 to 2 hours

Materials

Flip chart and markers; sticky notes or index cards

Purpose/Objectives

- To help a new team get clear on its values

- To provide anchors to team members during times of transition

Grouping

All team members

Warm-up

The leader explains that a new team is forming or that a new mission for the team has developed. The team is going through a transition period of moving from old values to new values.

Aerobics

1. Post three flip charts on the wall.
   Label them:

   "Good Old Days"
   "Keep"
   "Create New"

2. Ask the team members to write (on sticky notes or index cards) characteristics of the past, whether good or bad (one per note or card), large enough to be read from a distance.

3. Members post notes or cards on the flip chart labeled "Good Old Days."

4. Each person takes time to read what the others have written.

5. Team members ask for stories, clarifications.

6. Everyone decides which of the characteristics should be kept in the new environment.

7. Move those characteristics to the "Keep" chart.

8. Get consensus that all characteristics on the "Keep" chart are keepers. Will they serve in the new environment?

9. Now ask, "What's missing? What do we want to create for this new team?" Add these ideas to the "Create New" flip chart.

10. Select 6 to 8 new values. Divide into groups or use whole-team discussion to build a scenario to demonstrate that these new values are in place.

11. You may wish to burn or ceremoniously crumple and discard the "Good Old Days" chart.

12. Record and distribute the "Keep" and "Create" values and plan to revisit them at a later date.

Cooldown

Ask people if they were comfortable with this process. How did they feel about leaving the old and creating the new?

Note: This is a good exercise to use prior to building operating agreements.

Adapted from ideas from TEAMNET Newsgroup

Creating a Vision with Words

Workout Plan

When to use

After the team has determined its mission and goals, it's useful to create a vision that shows either the accomplishment of those goals or a vision of the team itself in action. You may choose to provide some baseline information for this exercise.

Time

2 hours

Materials

Creating a Vision with Words Worksheet
Flip charts and marking pens

Purpose/Objectives

- To create a common vision for the team, either in how it operates or its accomplishments

- To create a common image of what the team would like to become known for

Grouping

All team members

Warm-up

Explain that effective teams often have a vision for themselves that lifts them beyond the daily reality and that helps them to aspire to something more lofty that the day-to-day activities will contribute to.

Aerobics

1. Pick a point in the future. It may be the time of project completion or 3 to 5 years if it's an intact group.

2. Imagine the team is in a helicopter looking down over itself at a certain point in time.

   - What would they see?

   - Who would be their customers?

   - What would the customers be saying about them?

   - How would they interact with one another?

   - If it's the completion of a project, what would that project look like?

   - How would it be received?

   - Why is it special?

   - If it's an ongoing team, think about how they would be doing business.

3. Each person writes a one- to two-line vision on flip chart paper and posts it on the wall.

4. When everyone is finished, ask the team to list the common themes. Then ask them to choose one vision that particularly captured their imagination.

5. Write the chosen vision on a flip chart to be used as a starting point for the team's vision.

6. Ask people to pair up and discuss:

   - What needs to be added to make it look personal to their team?

   - What doesn't work for you?

7. In pairs, report their observations and make corrections to the vision.

8. Ask, If this were our vision for this team's future,

   - Would it inspire us?

   - Would we be proud to share it with others?

   - Could we commit to it?

9. Work through the question and the process until you gain consensus on the team's vision.

Cooldown

Decide what to do next. Should we let it settle and think about it? Are we ready to display it publicly? How can we best use this vision for ourselves and our work?

CREATING A VISION WITH WORDS WORKSHEET

The Helicopter View

1. What do we see?

2. Who are the customers?

3. What are they saying about us?

4. How do team members behave?

5. What do the end results look like?

6. How is it received by others?

7. Why is the outcome special?

8. Why is this team special?

Selection Interview

Workout Plan

When to use

At new team start-up. Replace departed team members or supplement team expertise.

Time

1 hour

Materials

Interview Questions Worksheet

Purpose/Objectives

- To find people who have different perspectives and skills

- To find people who are committed to the team's purpose

- To find people who have "fire in the belly"

- To find the best "athletes" for the team

Grouping

Team leader and prospective member. (Can also include all or selected other team members.)

Warm-up

Explain to the prospective team member that you are looking for a wide variety of people to work on your team. Explain whatever expectations or criteria that you have developed.

Aerobics

1. Use the suggested interview questions, plus others that are particularly applicable to your situation.

2. Explain the team you are putting together and its purpose, deliverables, and commitment involved.

3. At the conclusion of the interview, explain the process by which you will be selecting team members and when the person can expect to hear from you.

Cooldown

Code the information as it fits your requirements. Look for diversity in skills, attitudes, perspectives, and commitment to the team's purpose and process.

Discuss the positive aspects of the interviewees. Also, what areas are still in question? Do we believe that this person can contribute to the team? Is this a person we would like to work with? What new perspectives would he or she bring to the team?

Adapted from ideas from interviewees too numerous to mention

SELECTION INTERVIEW WORKSHEET

1. Tell me about your experiences with this type of team.

2. What kinds of expertise do you believe you could bring to the table?

3. How do you feel about working as a team? What makes a good team player?

4. Can you describe an instance where you had to challenge the ideas of others? Of the leader? What was the result?

5. Have you had any psychological profiles done? What was your profile?

6. If you were selected for this team, what would be a reward or recognition for you?

7. Describe a period where you worked under intense pressure? How did you react?

8. What are your questions about the team and its work?

9. Other questions specific to your situation.

Getting to Know You

Workout Plan

When to use

At the beginning of a new team or at the first meeting of that team. Although team members may know one another, they may need to get to know one another in a new context—that of this new team. Existing teams may use this exercise when new members join the team.

Time

1 hour (depending on the size of the team)

Materials

Getting to Know Your Team Interview Questions
Getting to Know You Worksheet

Purpose/Objectives

- To get to know each member quickly and in more depth

- To discover the skills and expertise present on the team

- To learn more about members' broader personalities

Grouping

All team members

Warm-up

Explain that this is a new team and that although you may know one another from past experiences, it is good to get the new team off on a well-grounded footing of mutual understanding.

Aerobics

1. Pass out the Getting to Know You Worksheet and allow members to read the questions.

2. Ask members to pair up and interview each other. (Suggest that they choose someone they don't know or don't know well). Give them 7 minutes each.

3. Each person introduces his or her partner to the rest of the group. Set a time limit based on the number of people in the group. (This exercise can take up to 30 minutes, but it will save hours in the long run because you will get everyone's background out in front of the group at one time.

Cooldown

What special commonalties did we hear? Are there any "holes" in experiences? What was a special purpose of this exercise? What questions should we have asked? How would you summarize this exercise? You may want to write your answers on a flip chart or white board.

Getting to Know Your Team Interview Questions

1. What is the name you prefer to be called? (Some people are called by names they prefer not to be called or will have stories about names they're called by friends and family.)

2. Where were you born? And where have you lived?

3. How long have you been with this organization? In what kinds of jobs? Other organizations?

4. What kinds of experiences have you had in working with teams? What positives? What could have been improved?

5. Why were you selected to this team? What expertise do you bring to the table for this team?

6. What's your favorite activity—outside the job?

7. What is it about you that no one in this room knows?

8. What is the one thing that anyone in this room might do that would make you most irritated?

9. What was the proudest moment in your life?

10. What do you hope will happen with this team?

GETTING TO KNOW YOU WORKSHEET

Name	Where from?	Work experience	Team experience	Selection

GETTING TO KNOW YOU WORKSHEET

Favorite activity	No one knows	Irritation	Proudest moment	Hopes

Basic Principles

Workout Plan

When to use
When the team is establishing the values and principles by which it will operate.

Time
1 to 2 hours

Materials
Basic Principles Worksheet
Flip charts and markers

Purpose/Objectives

- To develop a set of guiding principles by which the team wants to operate

Grouping
All team members

Warm-up
To guide our decision making and prioritize demands on our resources, we need to develop a set of basic principles that will define how we believe the team should operate. These principles will remind us and tell the world where we, as a team, stand.

Aerobics

1. Working alone, each person writes down a list of three principles or values he or she believes should be a team value or principle.

2. Record each principle, one at a time, round robin, until all principles are written on a flip chart.

3. Ask for questions, explanations, or clarification.

4. Combine or redefine those that are similar.

5. Prioritize the principles to a manageable list of five to ten basic principles.

6. Using the Basic Principles Worksheet, discuss the following:

   • "As evidenced by": Give examples from daily work that illustrate the application of this principle.

   • "Implications": What do we believe about this principle? How will it impact our work?

   • "At what price?" If we choose this principle, how much will it cost us in terms of time, energy, stress, or money?

   • "Next steps": What do we need to do further to integrate this principle into our work?

Cooldown
Are there too many principles? Not enough?
Where should we display these principles?
How can we keep them in the forefront of our thinking?

Adapted from suggestions by Michael Milano

BASIC PRINCIPLES WORKSHEET

	PRINCIPLES	Evidence	Implications	Price	Next Steps
1.					
2.					
3.					
4.					
5.					
6.					
7.					
8.					
9.					
10.					

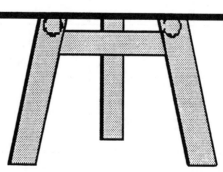

Basic Principles—Example

- Collaboration—not a place of individual work; everyone is involved for the benefit of each other and the client.

- We give clients the benefit of the doubt first.

- We treat people as equitably as possible.

- We are supportive of each other.

- We are honest in our communications.

- We won't take clients who violate our values.

- There is work we will turn down (belief the work will fail; concern about organization's commitment to the work).

- We focus on the objective.

- We try not to react to symptoms.

- We believe we can do business in ways that make money and attend to people.

Murphy & Milano, Inc.

Looking for Our Values

Workout Plan

When to use
Anytime in a team's life, but especially when the team wants to develop a set of shared values. These values can be used as a basis for operating agreements.

Time
$\frac{1}{2}$ to 1 hour

Materials
Writing surface and markers

Purpose/Objectives

- To examine our personal lives and what each of us values

Grouping
All team members

Warm-up
We all carry with us symbols of what we personally value.

Aerobics

1. Take out your wallet or purse, your pocket calendar, or anything else on you right now and see what you can find that may be a symbol of what is of value to you. Use both

perspectives: What do you see, and what values might that suggest? What do you find that shows the values you think you have?

2. Pick a partner and discuss what you found. For example, keys might be a symbol of the value for security. The customary behavior associated with security may be locking the car door every time you leave the car.

3. Each pair gives a quick example of some insight from this activity to the team.

Cooldown

How do our personal values relate to our team values? Are they the same? Different? What does this say about how we operate?

Adapted from Al Starkey

Start-Up—Example

<u>Our Values</u>

We believe the CUSTOMER COMES FIRST. Our commitment is to anticipate their needs and provide quality service that contributes to the success of our customers.

We will maintain an atmosphere of TRUST, HONESTY, and RESPECT, recognizing "People are Important," honoring the worth and dignity of each employee, customer, and stockholder.

We believe our EMPLOYEES ARE VALUABLE ASSETS. Through the Spirit of Teamwork, we will support employee development throughout the organization, acknowledge quality performance, and reward outstanding achievements.

We believe our responsibility to our stockholders is to UTILIZE SOUND MANAGEMENT OF FINANCIAL AND HUMAN RESOURCES. We will operate profitably to maintain a strong capital base to offset risks inherent in the industry. We will be progressive in developing innovative programs, promoting new ideas, and utilizing strategic planning to meet the evolving needs of our customers.

Farm Credit Services Southwest

Implementation Planning

Workout Plan

When to use
When the team is planning for implementation of a product or process in another part of the organization.

Time
Approximately 1 hour (depending on the size of the group and the complexity of the issue)

Materials
Implementation Planning Worksheet
Critique of Implementation Plan Worksheet
Flip chart for summarizing information

Purpose/Objectives

- To think through and plan for the implementation of products or processes developed by the team

- To request assistance or resources from other parts of the organization

Grouping
All team members

Warm-up
Ask each person to complete the Implementation Planning Worksheet.

Define a specific hand-off of product, request for resources, or other situations where you need the influence and support of others. ***Be sure to emphasize that discussion of the people to be influenced by the process must remain confidential and that this discussion should never leave the room.***

Aerobics

1. Answer each question on the worksheet, round robin.

2. Obtain consensus around each question. Ask for expert insight in regard to the person(s) to be influenced.

3. Given this profile, what is the best way to approach this person?

   - Who is the best person(s) to do this?

   - What support will they need?

Cooldown
Set a deadline and ask team members to put together the proposal. Plan for edits and oral dry runs prior to the presentation. Critique the plan using Critique of Implementation Plan Worksheet. Review the plan and execute.

IMPLEMENTATION PLANNING WORKSHEET

Issue/Problem/Request:

_____

_____

_____

1. Who do you need to influence?

2. What are their needs/wants?

3. How do they like to receive information?

   - Formally/informally?

   - On paper/in person?

   - From one person/a group?

   - Do they like it short and sweet?

   - Do they like it long and fully documented?

4. Which questions would they ask?

   - Who does this? Who is involved?

   - What is it?

   - Why should we do it?

   - How does it work?

   - How does it affect me, my group, the organization?

   - How much does it cost?

   - How much time will it take?

CRITIQUE OF IMPLEMENTATION PLAN WORKSHEET

Was the nature of the problem or recommendation clear?

Who is the intended audience for the presentation?

Is the presentation technique appropriate to the audience? Give specific reasons why or why not.

Did the presenter anticipate the questions his or her audience would ask? How?

How thoroughly did the presentation cover the problem and proposed solution? Did the presentation cover who, what, when, how, and why?

Was the documentation persuasive?

Other comments:

Meetings and Setting up the Rules

Workout Plan

When to use
At the beginning of a team's life or anytime when a team gets stuck on the process of its meetings.

Time
1 hour

Materials
Meeting Rules Worksheet
Flip chart and markers

Purpose/Objectives

- To develop agreements on meeting structure, content, facilitation, and format.

Grouping
All team members

Warm-up
Most teams do their collective work in meetings. It's important that these meetings be creative and productive. It's useful to develop agreements around how meetings will be structured and facilitated.

Aerobics

1. Label two flip chart pages:

   - "What I like about meetings"
   - "What I hate about meetings"

2. Brainstorm responses to each topic or have people walk around and write their responses under each heading.

3. Explain that we now have the opportunity to build agreements on how we will run our meetings.

4. Considering what was written on the charts, think about the questions on the Meeting Rules Worksheet and make notes.

5. Discuss each question and reach consensus on how this team will conduct its meetings.

6. Ask if any important issues have been omitted. Discuss those issues.

Cooldown

Ask members how they feel about their agreements. Find someone to record and pass out the agreements to each member. Explain that, if agreements are broken, the team will remind the person of the consensus agreement, or that agreement will be revisited to face possible amendment.

MEETING RULES WORKSHEET

1. Who will preside?

2. How will we set the agenda?

3. What should be the major content of meetings?

4. How often should we meet?

5. How long should we meet?

6. What if we get off track?

7. How can we build in some creativity to our meetings?

8. How do we make sure everyone is heard?

9. How should we make decisions?

   • If we decide on consensus, how will we work through objections to reach consensus?

10. Who or how will we check our meeting process?

11. Who will record minutes and action items?

12. How soon will they be distributed to members?

13. Who else needs to get copies of our minutes?

14. What other agreements do we need to make about meetings?

See
Example
Page

Meeting Agenda—Example

☐ Team

☐ Meeting

☐ Date

Topic (what)	Desired outcome/product	Approach (how)	Time (how long)	Leader (who)

Team Values to Agreements

Workout Plan

When to use
When the team is beginning and wants to build some agreements on how the team will operate together on the basis of shared values.

Time
1 hour or more

Materials
Flip chart paper and markers

Purpose/Objectives

- To explore our personal values around teams

- To provide a common base of shared values

- To translate these values into operating agreements for the team

Grouping
All team members

Warm-up
Explain that this team has the opportunity to build its own rules. Rules that are based on our personal values and experiences are ones that can best be remembered and followed.

Aerobics

1. Ask team members to think back through their lives to find a time when they participated on a team of some sort that they consider to be highly successful and highly rewarding. People tend to think in terms of sports teams. Remind them of other kinds of teams they may have been on, such as a school play, a volunteer group, a military experience, a family experience, a crisis where people quickly banded together, or a husband-wife experience.

2. Each team member tells her story to the group.

3. On a flip chart, list the characteristics of these successful team experiences.

4. What kind of values do these characteristics exemplify?

5. Select four to six values that each person can agree with.

6. Based on these characteristics, what kinds of agreements can we make to demonstrate these values?

7. Using the whole group or subgroups, develop a small set of operating agreements.

Cooldown

Assign a small group to clarify the agreements and the values. Plan to bring these documents back to the whole group at the next meeting.

Adapted from ideas by Peter Grazier

E. Continuous Improvement of Teams

INTRODUCTION

Continuous improvement was an important recurring theme with the team leaders. No matter how successful they were, they were always trying to improve their performance as a team and the achievements on their tasks—their business. Teamwork is an iterative process. Because we are human beings, there is always room to work on increasing our performance with customers, checking our direction, understanding each other, and planning for change.

> *We are all a work in progress: the school, the faculty, the teams, the students. It's never finished.*
> George Schumaker, Green Hedges School

TRAINING

Continuous improvement means continuous learning. Training was universal as a way to improve performance. The kind of training teams and members received was all over the board. Some examples are:

- Financial statements

- Quality improvement tools and techniques

- Communication

- Technology

- Teamwork

- Economics

- Future predictions in technology, transportation, or any relevant topic

- Personal finance

- Values clarification

- Balance sheets

- Feedback skills (giving and taking)

- Process improvement

- Money management

E *mpowering people without training is like giving a teenager the keys to the car without teaching them to drive.*

Terry Tierney, Allegro Coffee

T *here is a tremendous need for training. As usual, senior management underestimates the time and need for training. When you train people well, you give them more opportunities to become successful.*

Rich Herink, SuperTel Hospitality, Inc.

U *se outside consultants. Most of us are technicians. Don't be afraid to make a long-term investment in training. What if you train them and they leave? What if you don't train them and they stay?*

Gary Dyer, Southwest Farm Credit

CROSS-TRAINING

Another recurrent theme was the move from specialist to generalist. Everyone had to learn everyone else's job. The customer would have one phone number, and anyone would be able to answer the question. This cross-training was scary for some team members. They didn't know if they could do it and at the same time they were giving up their special technical skills to others; perhaps they might not feel as valued as they did the old way. Once they see they can do it, they're excited and pleased with themselves.

A *rrange creative scheduling. Don't forget peoples' main job. Don't ask someone to do something you wouldn't do.*

Jincy Fletcher, Flynn Elementary School

W *e believe in learning. You can use conflict as a catalyst. It's okay to be "raggedy," to not know everything or have your thoughts well-formed. We want people to be open-minded. Our motto is "Straight Talk," honest, direct communication.*

Judith H. Katz, Kaleel Jamison Consulting Group, Inc.

> *I* *see a team where everyone is concerned with the organization's success, the team's success, and each team member's success. When it gets out of balance, the team falls apart.*
>
> Jay Penick, Northwest Farm Credit Services

Again, team leaders advise **Patience.**

Provide a safe environment where mistakes can be made and provide support for the new learnings.

CONTINUOUS FEEDBACK

To provide continuous feedback to team members, many organizations used 360° feedback instruments. These instruments were filled out by the boss, peers, self, and subordinates, allowing members to see themselves as others see them. These instruments often became the basis for performance reviews.

The 360° feedback instruments were sometimes standardized, purchased products; others were companywide measures, or were developed by the team itself to measure the behaviors they believed to be important. The team-developed instruments were often based on the values adopted by the team.

> *W* *e do a 360° feedback with peers. Eventually we will bring in patients and their families. The more it's used, the more valuable it becomes.*
>
> Tracy Wagner, Menninger Clinic

> *L* *ong-term employees are hard to change. We use 360° feedback every six months. It works pretty well to change behavior. In our culture, we find it hard to confront and this tool makes it easier to give feedback. Some people are not team players. We coach, work out a plan, move people among units if necessary. Finally, it's change or exchange.*
>
> Jack Shuler, Pee Dee Farm Credit

> *W*hen conflict or performance problems happen, try to resolve it within the team. If you have taken it off-line, bring the issue back to the group so everyone knows what's going on. Follow through and bring it back, if it's a team issue.
>
> Joan Gotti, Chase Manhattan Bank

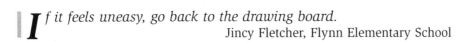

> *I*f it feels uneasy, go back to the drawing board.
>
> Jincy Fletcher, Flynn Elementary School

Customer feedback was another way the teams found to improve performance. Diverse methods were used here, including one-on-one interviews with customers and group focus interviews. Questionnaires on customer satisfaction provided input to the team. Other teams used corporate customer satisfaction questionnaires as a base and adapted them to their own products and services.

> *W*e wanted to improve our interaction with one important supplier. First we tried to map out what was working, where we needed to improve. Then we went to the supplier and said, "This is our view. We're not sure it's right." They did the same thing. We used the supplier scorecard and asked them to measure us as a customer. Measure us by what we do, not what we say. Let's rewrite the script and lay out a set of reasonable expectations.
>
> Gerrold Walker, Sun Microsystems

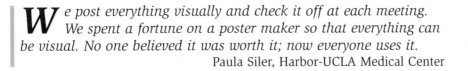

> *W*e post everything visually and check it off at each meeting. We spent a fortune on a poster maker so that everything can be visual. No one believed it was worth it; now everyone uses it.
>
> Paula Siler, Harbor-UCLA Medical Center

TWO MAJOR FRUSTRATIONS

For various reasons, *people get weary.* Weary in the context of being bone-tired, so burned out that a good night's sleep would not refresh them. In the excitement of the project and the synergy of the team, people overcommit, that is, beyond their physical and mental capacities. They want to do the job, but they run out of steam. Others are members of cross-functional teams who still have full-time jobs in their departments. Then the team's work sometimes felt like bearing extra duties, no matter how committed to the team's mission they were.

> *T*eam members usually get to a point where what they really want to accomplish falls in the "too tough" category. They don't want to stick their neck out, make a strong recommendation. It's important for the leader to say, "We just spent a whole bunch of time getting smart on this. Ours is probably the most informed opinion available. Let's tell them what we think, rather than waste the time we have invested."
>
> Emily Willey, Honeywell Inc.

> *T*here are too many issues, too many priorities, too many opportunities. You have to recognize it when it's going on. Just say it out loud.
>
> Tyler Johnston, Dreyer's Grand Ice Cream

> *T*here will be tough times. Step back. Look at the cost-benefit of working as a team. It has a price, but lower than not working as a team. Being accountable for others' success is tough.
>
> Michael Milano, Murphy & Milano, Inc.

Sometimes the team has to wait: wait for an approval, wait for the technology to catch up with them, or wait for all the parts to come together. This situation is problematic for the team and its leader. If one can anticipate where the weariness might come or just understand that it will arrive, the team members can make plans for ways to reenergize themselves and one another.

One of the best ways of dealing with this juncture is to acknowledge it: "We're tired and weary." Then, "What shall we do?"

> *P*eople get energized by strategy, looking at the big picture, new learnings, working on the future. A subgroup came to me, "We're getting tired." I wanted to say, "Let's take a break," but I did not. We couldn't stop or slow down. We went off to look at the big picture again, asking ourselves how can we do it easily, more efficiently. Where is the 80/20 break? You have to deal with it. This is normal.
>
> Anil Arora, The Pillsbury Company

The team becomes complacent. It's relatively easy to get creativity and innovation when what you've been doing no longer works, when you're going down the tubes. This is one of the most opportune times for a leader to step onto a bankrupt scene. People will "think outside the lines" and look to one another for help. Everyone wants the opportunity to succeed.

When the organization and the team are extraordinarily successful, it's harder to think creatively and become more innovative. "How can we do this better?" is one question to ask. "What else should we be doing?" is another question.

> *T**he most dangerous time in a pig's life is when he's fat.***
> Gary Dyer, Southwestern Farm Credit Services

> *M**ove the benchmark. Challenge each other to reach higher levels of performance. Get all ideas and thoughts on the table. A team gets to thinking in a box because it's comfortable. It's my job to move them outside their comfort zone.***
> Jay Penick, Northwest Farm Credit Services

> *T**he biggest challenge is inertia. When you're successful, it's hard, but essential, to keep looking for a way to do it better. Change is constant. If you're standing still, you're moving backwards.***
> Terry Tierney, Allegro Coffee

If continuous improvement is the watchword of the team, then complacency, just like weariness, can be confronted directly.

"Thinking outside the lines, outside the box," were expressions I heard from almost every team leader I interviewed. My best research shows that this expression comes from the work of James Adams (1974), who posited the problem of the nine dots: Draw no more than four straight lines (without lifting the pencil from the paper) that will cross through all nine dots.

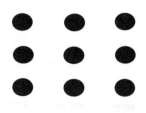

Possible answers are:

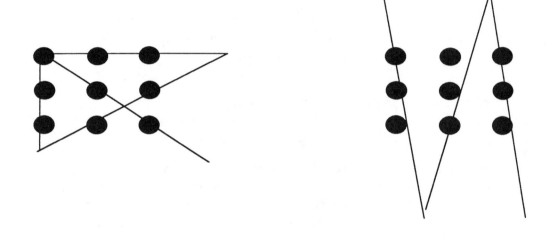

The point is that individuals and teams and organizations impose rules on themselves that aren't in the environment. Team leaders find this phenomenon frustrating. They want new ideas and creativity. The CEO's in particular were looking for new products and new processes.

All the team leaders were focused on continuous improvement of the team and the task. Working in teams was enormously satisfying despite occasional frustrations. Team leaders believed this team should be a role model to the rest of the organization.

I have to find ways to get people to think outside of the box. Find ways to make learning OK and safe.

Gerrold Walker, Sun Microsystems

*W*e see ourselves as a model for other teams. When decisions need to be made, we say "Put it through the process." It takes longer, but the decisions stick.

Dean Lehman, BancOne

*W*e want to model our values, what we think is important. We want to drive teamwork across the organization through our influence on others, to work with our colleagues so that everyone looks good. Build trust and partnership with others.

Joan Gotti, Chase Manhattan

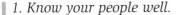

1. *Know your people well.*

2. *Help them set career objectives and help them get there.*

3. *Don't do their job for them.*

4. *Set aside your solution and accept theirs.*

5. *Teams are dynamic and my role changes daily.*

6. *Live in the field with your team.*

Rich McCool, Gulf Power Company

*T*he team was enormously clever. Everyone was creative in different ways. Equality and teamwork are not synonymous. Find people's strengths. We were bonded together by the highest purpose. It was an honor to be involved. Gradually, they let go of the need to work independently.

Name withheld upon request

*C*elebrate. Be creative, not hokey celebrations. Celebrate personal and team victories.

Name withheld upon request

Note: The exercises that follow this section of the book focus on the problems facing the team and give you some ideas for energizing your team. The energizers are coded with a spark plug, like in the example below.

ENERGIZER

Example of
energizer device.

The Voice of the Customer

Workout Plan

When to use
If continuing improvement is the watchword of a successful team, then continuous feedback from the team's customers is necessary.

Time
1 to 2 hours (plus pilot test)

Materials
Flip chart and markers

Purpose/Objectives

- To design a format for customer feedback

- To decide how the form will be used: face-to-face, focus groups, or questionnaires

- To decide who will be the recipient of the feedback form

Grouping
Can be a subset of the team

Warm-up
Explain that almost every firm, school, health care facility, and so on uses customer satisfaction surveys. These surveys help pinpoint the areas for improvement. If you are a team with internal

customers, perhaps you can adapt the questionnaire that's used by your firm for external customers.

Aerobics

1. Who is the customer? What do we want to know about the product? What do we want to know about our service to them? Think about the products and service we provide.

Product quality is:

- Consistent and conforms to specifications

- Useful to the customer

- Easy to use

- Gives value for the money

Service quality is:

- Reliability: The ability to provide what was promised, dependably and accurately

- Assurance: The knowledge and courtesy of employees and their ability to convey trust and confidence

- Tangibles: The physical facilities and equipment and the appearance of personnel

- Empathy: The degree of caring and individual attention provided to customers

- Responsiveness: The willingness to help customers and provide prompt service

Adapted from research by Berry, et al (1989)

2. Try to build one question or statement for each dimension. Although open-ended questions give you the richest data, people who are very busy will not take the time to answer your questions. A combination of numerical ratings and open questions is best.

3. Decide how you will use your questionnaire: face-to-face, individually, focus groups, or sent out.

4. Decide who will be the recipients of your feedback form.

5. Decide who you can pilot your survey on.

6. Plan for distribution.

Cooldown
Plan to revisit this exercise at a specified date to share the results of the surveys.

Adapted from ideas from Roger Shaffer

Client Service Survey—Example

Please mark the appropriate column to express your reaction to the following statements about our firm.

	Strongly Agree	Agree	Disagree	Strongly Disagree
Our firm seems familiar with your problems.	_____	_____	_____	_____
We handle your work on a timely basis.	_____	_____	_____	_____
Your phone calls are returned promptly.	_____	_____	_____	_____
Partners and staff are available when needed.	_____	_____	_____	_____
Tax returns and other documents look professional.	_____	_____	_____	_____
Filing instructions for tax returns are clear.	_____	_____	_____	_____
Fees are reasonable for the services rendered.	_____	_____	_____	_____
We keep you informed of changes in the tax law.	_____	_____	_____	_____
Our tax planning advice is appropriate and timely.	_____	_____	_____	_____
You have benefited from our advice.	_____	_____	_____	_____
We follow up to help you implement suggested advice.	_____	_____	_____	_____
Our staff appears to be technically competent.	_____	_____	_____	_____

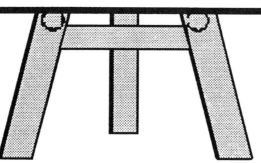

Our firm always treats
you courteously.   _____   _____   _____   _____

Our firm appears to be
well-managed.   _____   _____   _____   _____

                                                         YES   NO

Would you recommend our firm to others?
If no, why not? _____
_____

May we use you as a reference?
Do you have any unmet business or tax-related
needs with which we could help?
If yes, please explain: _____
_____

Has our firm ever failed you in any way?
If yes, please explain: _____
_____

Would you recommend any changes in the way we
do business?
Please describe: _____
_____

Would you like more information on any of our
services?
Please list: _____
_____

General Comments: _____
_____

**Please return this survey by folding and securing it and dropping it
in the mailbox. Thank you.**
Your name (optional)

_____

Coet & Coet, P.C., Certified Accountants

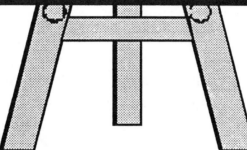

What Will People Say?

Workout Plan

When to use
In the team start-up or at other points in the team's life. Many teams believe they should be a model to others. This exercise can help them assess their performance in this area.

Time
1 to 2 hours

Materials
Flip chart and markers

Purpose/Objectives

- To introduce new concepts in strategic planning

- To provide a basis for developing a vision for the team

- To provide a vehicle for self-critique

Grouping
All team members

Warm-up
This exercise is designed to try to see ourselves as we would like others to see us. We'll examine our team from various points of view.

Aerobics

1. Identify the groups of people who are related to your teams and who have interest in your team. These can be other teams, employees, upper management, the board of directors, stakeholder groups, customers, and so on.

2. List each group at the top of a separate piece of flip chart paper and post on the walls.

3. Ask participants to imagine that they are at a party where people are saying the things about them that they wish and hope other people would say.

4. Have them write a list of what those people are saying about them on each chart. (Emphasize that this is what you **want** them to be saying about you.)

5. Review each chart:

   - Discuss to clarify any comments that are unclear

   - Discuss to merge those comments that are essentially the same

   - Prioritize the list and see what desired perceptions rise to the top

Cooldown

How are we doing with each stakeholder group? How can we use this information in building a strategic plan or vision or a plan for continuous improvement?

Adapted from ideas by Michael Milano

Creating a Vision with Pictures
What Is? What Should Be?

Workout Plan

When to use
When the team has been in operation for some time, wants to create a vision or a new vision for itself, or wants to redirect its efforts.

Time
1 to 2 hours

Materials
Flip chart, markers, and tape

Purpose/Objectives

- To determine how the rest of the world sees this team

- To create a new vision for the team

Grouping
All team members

Warm-up
Explain that we are going to think about how the rest of the world (the organization and customers) sees this team. Then you are going to describe how this team wants to be seen by its stakeholders. Then we'll plan for how to make our new vision come true.

Aerobics

1. Each team member gets one sheet of flip chart paper, plus markers of various colors.

2. On the top of the paper, members draw a picture of how they believe various stakeholders (management, customers, or suppliers) see them in their current situation.

3. On the second half of the paper, each member draws a picture of what they wish were true—what they wish others would think of them.

4. Post the pictures around the room, with the current situation showing and the desired situation covered up.

5. Each member observes the other's work.

6. What are the themes we see in all these pictures? Write on a flip chart labeled "Current."

7. Now show the desired vision for the team.

8. Each member explains her own picture.

9. What are the themes we see in these pictures? Write these themes on the flip chart labeled "Vision."

10. Try to summarize the vision. Pick out key words and points to make.

11. Assign a few team members to "wordsmith" the vision statement.

12. Decide when to revisit the new clean statement of vision.

Cooldown

Plan to revisit the vision and determine the necessary action steps to make it a reality.

Weighted Decision Analysis

Workout Plan

When to use
When the team is stuck on a difficult decision or when it is hard to gain consensus.

Time
1 to 2 hours (depending on the complexity of the problem)

Materials
Weighted Decision Analysis Worksheet
Flip chart or white board and sticky notes

Purpose/Objectives

- To help the team arrive at a decision on a difficult and complex issue with many feasible alternatives

Grouping
All team members affected by the decision

Warm-up
Explain that the team has reached a point where a decision needs to be made on a complex issue. We will now use a more structured quantitative approach that can help clarify our thinking.

Aerobics

1. Identify the decision that needs to be made.

2. List the possible alternatives. Narrow choices to no more than four.

3. What are the requirements for this decision? What are the "must-haves"? Try to limit "musts" to a manageable number.

4. What are the "wants," that is, the desirable attributes of a decision? List these under "wants."

5. On a scale of 1 to 10, weight the necessity of each "want."

6. Test each alternative against the "musts" and the "wants."

   - If the alternative fails the "musts" list, discard it.

   - If the alternative meets the "musts" list, then weigh the ability of the alternative to meet the "wants."

7. Multiply the weighting by the ability to meet the "wants."

8. Total the score for each alternative. The highest score should fulfill the "musts" and most of the "wants."

Cooldown

Ask the team if everyone agrees that this is the most desirable alternative. If they do not, go back and check your "wants" list and the weightings you gave to each one. Also, check to ensure that any "musts" or "wants" haven't been omitted. Reach agreement and support for the decision.

WEIGHTED DECISION ANALYSIS WORKSHEET

What is the decision?					
Alternatives		Alternative 1	Alternative 2	Alternative 3	Alternative 4
MUST-Requirements (mandatory, realistic)					
1.					
2.					
3.					
WANT (desirable)	**Wt.**				
1.					
2.					
3.					
4.					
5.					
6.					
7.					
8.					
9.					
10.					
TOTAL					

Continuous Improvement Exercise No. **5**   **Direction**

Bottled Lightning

Workout Plan

When to use
To break out of the mold of ordinary ways of doing things and to capture ideas from other companies and teams and adapt them to your own situation.

Time
Several weeks (but only a few hours a day)

Materials
As needed

Purpose/Objectives

- To develop a new paradigm, process, product, or service

Grouping
Designated team members (usually a set team)

Warm-up
Explain that it is unnecessary to reinvent the wheel every time we want to change something or create some new product or process for our team. There are many companies or other teams who have developed similar products or processes. We plan to study their work, capture the best parts, and adapt them to our team.

Aerobics

1. Decide on the desired product or process.

2. Decide on other companies or teams to investigate.

3. Develop questions to ask others.

4. Interview others.

5. Study the results and decide which aspects seem to be best suited to our team.

6. Adapt and integrate the best practices from others into the team's new product or process.

Cooldown

After adapting the new practice, test it with other interested stakeholders. Ask, are there other products or processes that can be improved in a similar way?

Adapted from ideas of Terry Tierney

PROBLEM OR PROCESS OR PRODUCT TO BE STUDIED WORKSHEET

Results of Investigation

Company A	Company B	Company C	Company D
_____	_____	_____	_____
_____	_____	_____	_____
_____	_____	_____	_____
_____	_____	_____	_____
_____	_____	_____	_____

What are the best ideas from each company?

_____

_____

_____

_____

How can we adapt them to improve our own team?

Bottled Lightning—Example

1. Desired product: new-employee handbook

2. Identify other companies and investigate their new-employee handbooks

3. Interview (sample questions?)

4. Study results and determine best-suited aspects

Company A

Company B

Company C

Company D

ADAPT

Strategic 360° Feedback

Workout Plan

When to use
When the team is looking to improve individual and/or team performance.

Time
1 to 2 hours (plus follow-up)

Materials
Copy of the Strategic Plan <u>or</u> copy of the team's operating agreements <u>or</u> other relevant standards of performance.
Flip charts and markers

Purpose/Objectives

- To provide feedback for individual growth and improvement.

- To provide benchmark data to track continuous improvement.

- To provide behavioral descriptions of abstract traits and values.

Grouping
All team members

Warm-up

In order to track our progress toward our goals, provide feedback to each other, and make our standards for performance real, we'll develop our own 360° peer review form.

Aerobics

1. Choose the areas where you want to track progress.

   • Is it a strategic plan?

   • The team's vision for itself?

   • The team's values?

   • The team's operating agreements?

   • The team's critical success factors?

2. Select a manageable number to track. 5 to 10 standards.

3. In sub-groups, write 3 to 5 behavioral descriptions of each standard. Say to yourself, if we were demonstrating _ _ _ _ _ _ (integrity, for example), What would it look like?

4. Bring descriptions back to the group and critique each one.

   • Is it clear?

   • Could we see it?

   • Is it sufficient?

   • Do we agree that these descriptions adequately describe the behaviors we would like to see?

Cooldown

After you reach a consensus, type it up and pass it around for further study. Pilot the format and see where it works and where the "bumps" are.

Note: The leader may wish to be the guinea pig.

Adapted from ideas by Jack Shuler

**For Example
See**

**Peer Performance
Review**

Page 136

Peer Performance Review—Example

Comments: Please place comment in the space provided in appropriate category.

1. Unacceptable   2. Meets expectations some of the time (50% or less)
3. Meets expectations   4. Exceeds expectations 50% of the time
5. Consistently exceeds expectations

Score of 1 or 5 requires a comment

	a) Integrity	b) Responsibility	c) Attitude	d) Professionalism	e) Customer Focus	f) Dependable, Reliable, Consistent
	1. Trustworthy 2. Keeps information confidential 3. Displays uncompromising honesty	1. Willing to be accountable for work 2. Takes ownership for work responsibilities 3. Willing to risk and think "outside" the box 4. Sets and maintains high work standards	1. Offers assistance to help rescue issues not specifically assigned 2. Provides help and shares responsibility for outcome 3. Willing to deal with special requests 4. Easy to do business with	1. Conducts self in business-like manner in front of customer. 2. Displays admirable behaviors of a business owner 3. Serves as an ambassador for association, internally and externally	1. Never looses sight of who the customer is 2. Strives to exceed customer expectations	1. Provides service that is promised 2. Consistent in service delivery 3. Can be counted on to follow through on projects 4. Delivers accurate input
Name	**Performance** High . . . . Low 5 4 3 2 1 N/A **Comments**	**Performance** High . . . . Low 5 4 3 2 1 N/A **Comments**	**Performance** High . . . . Low 5 4 3 2 1 N/A **Comments**	**Performance** High . . . . Low 5 4 3 2 1 N/A **Comments**	**Performance** High . . . . Low 5 4 3 2 1 N/A **Comments**	**Performance** High . . . . Low 5 4 3 2 1 N/A **Comments**

Provided by Pee Dee Farm Credit

360° Debrief

Workout Plan

When to use
After receiving 360° feedback from peers, boss, or subordinates

Time
One hour alone, one hour in the group

Materials
360° Debrief Worksheet

Purpose/Objectives

- To provide a format for examining peer's and other's feedback

- To help put the data into manageable perspective

Grouping
Individual and all team members

Warm-up
After receiving peer or other feedback it is necessary to contemplate the meaning of the information you have received. After personal, individual study, each member can decide which parts of the feedback he/she chooses to share with others.

Aerobics

1. Using the Debrief Worksheet, study your results and answer the questions.

2. After study, decide which parts of the information you wish to share with the group.

3. If there is a composite profile of the group, this should be presented first. Then each person can see how his/her individual profile compares to the group.

4. Discuss the group profile.

5. Each person should share the following:

    *   What pleased me?

    *   What I don't understand. Can someone give me an example?

    *   What I will not change

    *   What I will change

    *   What kind of help I may need from the group in order to make changes.

Cooldown

Discuss any special or unexpected things that were heard. Ask if there is any follow-up that needs to occur. What was the particular value of this feedback? When should we do it again? (6 to 12 months are recommended.)

Adapted from ideas by Pauline Russell

360° DEBRIEF WORKSHEET

	GROUP	SELF

1. What pleased me?

2. What surprised me?

3. What don't I understand?

4. What I cannot/will not change.

5. What I will change.

6. What kinds of help/action do I need to make the change?

7. Other comments:

Communication Networks

Workout Plan

When to use

When the team is stuck in communication methods. When you want to jolt the creativity level.

Time

Approximately 1 hour

Materials

Deck of Cards

Index cards or sticky notes

Flip chart and markers

Purpose/Objectives

- To analyze our current communication networks and how we can improve them

- To determine gaps and inefficiencies

Grouping

All team members

Warm-up

In the spirit of continuous improvement of our team, we're going to try an experiment in how we tend to communicate with each other. We're going to look at some of our assumptions dealing with communication and make plans for improvement.

Aerobics

1. The facilitator will assign each of the four communications networks, in sequence, to the group to solve a problem involving playing cards.

2. Only the face cards (kings, queens, and jacks) and aces will be used, making a total of 16 playing cards. Deal the cards to each person until all of them are dealt. Not everyone will have the same number of cards. The facilitator will pocket one card.

   The problem is to determine which card is missing as quickly as possible and notify all group members. If the group is large, use more cards from the deck.

3. Read the rules or pass them around.

4. Solve the problem using each communication network in sequence: the chain, the wheel, and the circle. Time each round.

5. When you reach network #4, announce that all the rules are off. Disregard the rules.

Cooldown

Which communication network allowed us to solve the problem quickly and accurately? What was the satisfaction of group members with the different problem-solving processes? Did some members experience more satisfaction than others? What happened when we reached exercise #4? What can we learn/change from this exercise? How do we normally communicate?

Background Note:

Organizations typically establish communications channels or networks to control and limit the type and amount of information that can flow through the different levels. In large organizations especially, chaos would result if every employee could freely communicate with every other employee up to and including the administrator. Pictured on pg. 143 are four typical types of communication networks. The arrows represent the lines of communication that are open to members of the team.

Note that the wheel and chain are more centralized communication networks while the circle and free communication networks are less centralized. For relatively simple problems, centralized communication networks generally result in faster and more accurate decisions. With less structured problems, open or less centralized communication networks work better.

On the other hand, satisfaction of team members is higher with open communication networks and lower with centralized communication networks.

COMMUNICATION NETWORKS EXERCISE

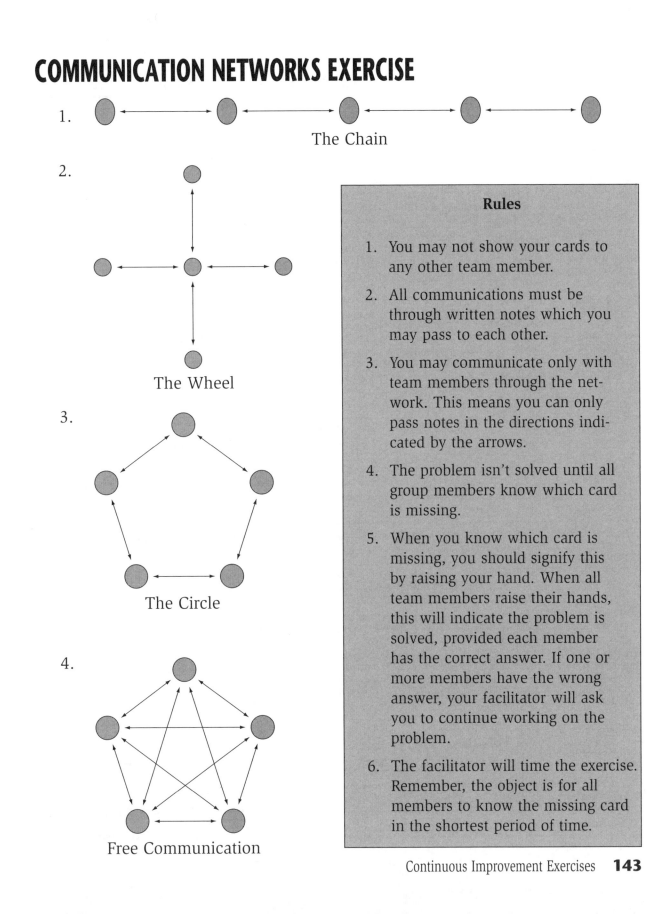

1.

The Chain

2.

The Wheel

3.

The Circle

4.

Free Communication

Rules

1. You may not show your cards to any other team member.

2. All communications must be through written notes which you may pass to each other.

3. You may communicate only with team members through the network. This means you can only pass notes in the directions indicated by the arrows.

4. The problem isn't solved until all group members know which card is missing.

5. When you know which card is missing, you should signify this by raising your hand. When all team members raise their hands, this will indicate the problem is solved, provided each member has the correct answer. If one or more members have the wrong answer, your facilitator will ask you to continue working on the problem.

6. The facilitator will time the exercise. Remember, the object is for all members to know the missing card in the shortest period of time.

Continuous Improvement Exercise No. **9**

Let's Read a Book

Workout Plan

When to use
At any time in the team's life

Time
$\frac{1}{2}$ day

Materials
Book
Let's Read a Book Worksheet
Flip chart paper and markers

Purpose/Objectives

- To provide new perspectives to the team's work

- To provide a common language

- To provide new learning for all

Grouping
All team members

Warm-up
Discuss the last time the members learned something new. Most people will tell about their experiences rather than about studying and learning. Explain that we are going to select a book and each of us will read it, discuss it, and adapt the teachings to our team.

Gather ideas for one book to read. (Suggestions can be recent books on management or business, technology, interpersonal skills, or whatever interests the team.)

Aerobics

After reading the book:

1. Ask each person to discuss: What was most important to you? What did you learn that was new? Did you disagree with any parts of the book?

2. Summarize the responses on a flip chart.

3. Now, taking what we have learned from this book, what parts are especially applicable to our work?

4. Choose one or two ideas to implement immediately.

5. Choose one or two ideas that merit further study.

Cooldown
Discuss the process of learning "by the book." Would we like to do this again? How can we make it more valuable?

Adapted from ideas by Gerrold Walker

LET'S READ A BOOK WORKSHEET

Title of Selected Book: _____

1. What was most important?

2. What did you learn that was new?

3. What was unclear to you?

4. Did you disagree with anything?

5. How can we adapt this new learning to our team?

The Huddle

Workout Plan

When to use
Any time someone on the team needs an update or input. Some teams have a regularly scheduled huddle, say, Monday morning at 9:00 A.M.

Time
15 minutes

Materials
None

Purpose/Objectives

- To update team members on schedules, upcoming dead-lines, or other significant milestones

- To get immediate input on a topic, client, and/or issue

- To prioritize projects or pieces of projects for the next week or two (**not** to problem solve, brainstorm, or work on marketing or deeper issues)

Grouping
All team members who are present in the office

Warm-up

Any team member can call a huddle at any time: "I need a huddle." The person who called the huddle states his or her needs for help or information.

Aerobics

Team members do a "go 'round." Each member shares information at the macrolevel regarding the reason for the huddle.

If it is a regularly scheduled huddle to update members on progress, the team does a "go 'round" on schedules, priorities, and what they're doing. Each member has 2 to 4 minutes to report.

Cooldown

Record action steps if necessary. Break into minihuddles with colleagues if problem solving or more in-depth discussion on specific issues is required.

Adapted from ideas by David Hannegan

If This Team Were a _ _ _ _ _

Workout Plan

When to use
At various points in the team's life when they need to critique themselves and rise to a higher level of performance.

Time
1 to 2 hours

Materials
If This Team Were a _ _ _ _ _ Worksheet
Flip charts and markers

Purpose/Objectives

- To look at ourselves and our team as a whole

- To provide continuous improvement

- To create ideas and to be imaginative as well as analytical

Grouping
All team members

Warm-up
Explain that as the team performs, we get into habits and norms of how things are done. Today we're going to examine ourselves and see what areas to continue in and what areas to improve on.

Aerobics

1. Each person completes the sentences found on the If This Team Were a _ _ _ _ _ Worksheet.

2. Discuss each perception one at a time, round robin.

3. Ask these questions, then post the answers:

    •   What themes did we hear?

    •   What do we like and want to keep?

    •   What surprised us?

    •   What do we believe is true and wish it weren't true?

    •   If we could make one change in our team's work, what would it be?

4. Record the themes, the strengths, and the desired changes.

5. Decide what, if anything, the team would like to do as a result of this exercise.

Cooldown

Summarize the activities and plan to revisit the results at a stated date.

Adapted from ideas by Michael Milano

IF THIS TEAM WERE A _ _ _ _ _ WORKSHEET

If our team were a movie, we would be _ _ _ _ _ because

If our team were a song, we would be _ _ _ _ _ because

If our team were a game, we would be _ _ _ _ _ because

If our team were a book, we would be _ _ _ _ _ because

If our team were a store, we would be _ _ _ _ _ because

If our team were a sport, we would be _ _ _ _ _ because

If our team were a famous corporation, we would be _ _ _ _ _ because

If our team were in a department store, we would be in the _ _ _ _ _ department because

The possibilities are endless. The idea is to engage creativity and imagination with analytical thinking.

The exercise can be turned into visioning exercises by simply asking the same questions with a different focus. For example, if the team were operating the way you'd like to, what movie would you be and why?

Alien Consultants

Workout Plan

When to use
When the team wants to critique itself and its performance. At any time in the team's life, but after it has been working together for a while. This can also be used as values clarification exercise.

Time
1 to 2 hours

Materials
Flip chart and markers

Purpose/Objectives

- To provide a jump-start out of complacency

- To see ourselves as others see us

- To identify unspoken values and beliefs that undergird team functioning

Grouping
All team members. You may wish to divide into subgroups for different aspects of the exercise and report back to the whole team.

Warm-up
Explain that it's easy to become complacent, especially when things are going well. It's good to step back and look at ourselves from a different point of view.

Aerobics

1. Pretend that we are a group of aliens visiting our team and making observations so we can make a report to the mother ship. Here is what we are to report:

   - Values of these people (provide evidence from your observations)

   - Beliefs

   - Customs

   - Rituals

   - Decision making

2. Think about some day-to-day things that we do that could lead others to make assumptions about our values. For example, employees in some organizations appear to have a belief that if they write something down and distribute it, people will actually do what it says. The evidence is that people e-mail like crazy, say things like "I copied you on that," and appear to be frustrated that others are not doing what they are writing.

3. Report back to the whole team.

4. Is this the culture of our team?

5. What do we like about it?

6. If we could change one thing about this report, what would it be? How can we make that change happen?

Cooldown

Record the main points—good and bad—from the reports. Plan to revisit these at a later date.

Adapted from Michael Milano

Continuous Improvement Exercise No. **13** **Accountability**

Look At All the Angles

Workout Plan

When to use
When the team is stuck on a problem or needs to refine its direction and priorities or when the team is anticipating influencing another person in the organization.

Time
1 hour

Materials
Look at All the Angles Worksheet
Flip chart and markers

Purpose/Objectives

- To provide different perspectives to a particular problem

- To help the team think "outside the box"

Grouping
All members of the team affected by the issue under discussion

Warm-up
Explain that the team seems to be stuck on a particular issue. Today, you will try to approach the problem from several angles by imagining that team members are various people who will speak to the issue.

Aerobics

1. Define the problem or issue that you want to work on.

2. Brainstorm ideas for different people to comment on the issue.

3. Decide on three to five people. Think about these types:

   - Someone who is eternally optimistic

   - Someone who will be the devil's advocate

   - Someone who knows nothing about the issue

   - Someone who will nitpick

   - Someone who will agree, no matter what

   - Someone who is very creative

   - Someone who is obstinate and who hates change

4. "Role play" what you think each person would say about the problem.

5. Note the aspects of each person's point of view that seem worth pursuing further.

6. Determine what new insights have been gained from this exercise.

IDEAS
Bill Cosby
Bill Clinton
Bill Gates
Bill Murray
Billy Jean King
Billy Crystal
Madonna
Barbara Bush
Janet Reno
George Bush
George Burns
Boy George
Georgia O'Keeffe

Cooldown

Determine the next steps on this issue. Do we need more information from others? Can we decide now? Are we close to consensus?

LOOK AT ALL THE ANGLES WORKSHEET

1. Angle #1

2. Angle #2

3. Angle #3

4. Angle #4

5. Angle #5

Assault on Everest

Workout Plan

When to use

The team is planning a long and difficult project or process where there may be waits and times of stress. This is a plan for how to conserve their energy at various points and reenergize at other points.

Time

1 to 2 hours

Materials

Assault on Everest Scenario
Assault on Everest Worksheet
Flip chart and markers

Purpose/Objectives

- To prepare for a long and difficult project

- To prepare for times when team members will get weary and perhaps discouraged

Grouping

All team members

Warm-up

Explain the process that is before the team, that we will need to prepare in advance for our reaching the summit of Everest and our completion and implementation of the project. Explain that there will be times when we all get weary and tired and that we need to plan for ways to help one another through the tough times.

Aerobics

1. Have everyone look at the Assault on Everest Scenario.

2. Then look at the Assault on Everest Worksheet.

3. Mark out the times when certain projects, plans, or activities need to be in place to help each other through the project.

4. Discuss and brainstorm what needs to happen at various points in the climb to the summit.

5. Discuss and brainstorm where we think the difficult parts will come and how we can work through them.

Cooldown

Decide on an action plan (which may need to be amended) for accomplishing the "sticky points" in reaching the summit. Ask how members feel about the project, having anticipated some of the more difficult aspects.

Adapted from ideas by Jack Snider
Technical input from Ed Webster

Assault on Everest Scenario

To climb Mt. Everest, one starts in Kathmandu, where all the preparation with the locals are made. Then one walks or flies to Lukla and begins the trek on the "Everest Highway" to Namche Bazaar, then to Thengboche Monastery. At this point, real climbers are separated from trekkers. Climbers go to Periche and then to Base Camp. There are normally four camps between Base Camp and the summit. One must spend a great deal of time in base camp (sometimes two weeks to two months) acclimatizing. There are two dangerous places on the route—an icefall between Base Camp and Camp 1 and the summit.

When planning to reach the summit of Mt. Everest, a great deal of planning is involved.

1. One must deal with the logistics, food, water, and transportation.

2. Careful selection of the team and its support is necessary. A dependable leader who will work with the local people, the sherpas and porters, and the management is very important.

3. The team has a vision and a mission. "The only successful expedition is one where everyone gets out alive." This mission is to get everyone safely to the top and home again.

4. Determine the strengths and weaknesses everyone brings to the mountain—that is, experience, strength, talent, and wisdom.

5. Determine the core values. "We will sacrifice all for what? To reach the summit or leave a buddy to die? When push comes to shove, what gives?"

6. How will we energize one another when we are really tired and weary?

If we don't make it to the top, what will be our measure of success?

Think of your journey as a new route in your organization.

Plot out what happens en route and think about how you will help one another at each stage—in Kathmandu, Base Camp (long wait), Camp 1, Camp 2, Camp 3, Camp 4, and the summit.

- How is this scenario like the road ahead of the team?

- What preparations must be made?

- What milestones? With technical support from . . ?

- What will we do when we must wait?

- How will we energize one another when we are weary?

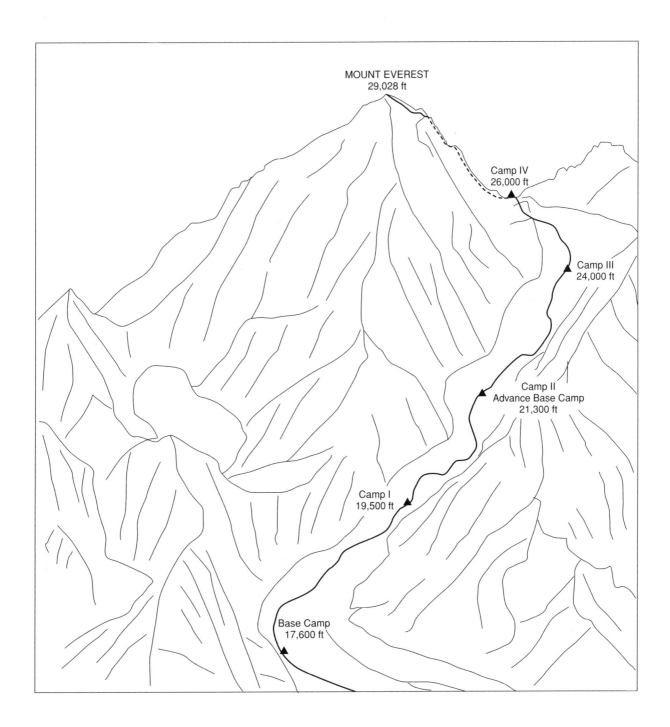

MOUNT EVEREST
29,028 ft

Camp IV
26,000 ft

Camp III
24,000 ft

Camp II
Advance Base Camp
21,300 ft

Camp I
19,500 ft

Base Camp
17,600 ft

ASSAULT ON EVEREST WORKSHEET

Preplanning

Base Camp

Camp 1

Camp 2

Camp 3

Camp 4

Summit

F. Saying Good-Bye

INTRODUCTION

Eventually, almost all project teams come to an end. The project is over—complete. Other teams will continue, such as a senior management or department team. By and large, most teams, for one reason or another, dissolve.

The team members often stay in touch with one another. Team leaders report that they check in on results of the team's efforts. They continue to monitor a new process.

- Is it being used?

- Does it need fine-tuning?

- Is it doing what we had hoped for it?

It's their baby, and they want to see it grow and prosper.

Sometimes, after a team is dissolved, a team leader will put out a call for help. Members respond immediately. "They pop up like toast."

Not every team experience is a good one. Even so, I recommend some kind of exercise to help the team members find new wisdom that they can apply to a new situation.

"Direction" is missing from the fitness menu in this chapter for obvious reasons; however, by reviewing the team's activities, one can help ensure improved team experiences in the future. These exercises can provide direction to help members on a new team.

HOW TO DISBAND THE TEAM

There's a certain amount of nostalgia involved when a team's work is complete. The synergy of the team and everyone working over their heads is energizing. They may have fond memories of how they worked together and how each member contributed to the whole.

Here are some ideas leaders described about disbanding a team:

- Hold a "wake." Have everyone tell a story about what they enjoyed and will remember most.

- Put people in teams to create skits to re-create (à la Saturday Night Live) experiences you've had together.

- Yearbook: Give each person a blank book for others to write in, to attach pictures to, or to draw in.

- Award medals, as in the Olympics.

- Create funny but relevant Participation Certificates.

- Give each person an award that pertains to their contribution to the team (a spark plug, a dictionary, a magnifying glass, and so on).

- Go out to dinner (and, as one leader said, "Do significant damage to the wine list.").

SUMMARY

Give a roast, give a toast but end with some fun activities to bring closure to a memorable event in each team member's work life.

Adapted from ideas by Darcy Hitchcock, Jack Shuler, and Seneca Murley

Closure Exercise No. **1**

Customer Focus

What Have We Accomplished?

Workout Plan

When to use
At the end of a project or special team effort. When the team members want to celebrate their accomplishments and learn from their experiences.

Time
About 1 hour

Materials
Flip chart paper and markers

Purpose/Objectives

- To debrief the team's work or project from the point of view of the customer

- To celebrate the things the team did well and to learn from past performance

Grouping
All team members

Warm-up
Explain that the work of the team is completed. In order to derive the most benefit from our experiences over the past time period, we will go back and look at our customers' perceptions of the team.

Closure Exercises **167**

Aerobics

1. Write the following on a flip chart:

   "I am pleased that this team . . ."

   "I wish this team had . . ."

2. Generate a list of customers of the team. Ask team members to volunteer to speak for each of the customers. The "customers" sit around a table or in a line in the front of the room. Ask each customer representative to complete the two sentences (above) you've posted.

3. Encourage questions from the group and the customer panel.

4. Discuss what the team could do differently in a new situation.

Cooldown

Summarize the main points under each question on the flip chart. Ask if this accurately reflects the conclusions of the customer panel. Discuss how each person can use this information in the future.

Note: Instead of guessing what various customers might say about the team, perhaps you can bring in several customers and invite them to talk about their experiences with the team.

Peer Recognition Poster

Workout Plan

When to use
When the team is dissolving, after a particularly meaningful session, or to celebrate each other's contributions.

Time
30 minutes (depending on the size of the group)

Materials
Flip chart paper and markers

Purpose/Objectives

- To provide peer recognition to individual team members

Grouping
All team members

Warm-up
Explain that the purpose of the exercise is to celebrate each person's contribution to the team and its success.

Aerobics

1. Pass out one sheet of flip chart paper and a different color marking pen to each team member.

2. Each team member writes his or her name at the top of the sheet of paper and posts the paper to the wall.

3. Each team member walks around the room and writes a statement about that person on the posted paper. The statement must be honest and from the heart.

4. Each team member writes on each person's poster.

5. Everyone silently reads everyone else's posters.

6. Each member takes down his or her own poster to use as he or she sees fit.

Cooldown
Ask what impact this exercise had on you personally, round robin.

Prouds and Regrets

Workout Plan

When to use

When the team is dissolving and wants to debrief its experiences of working together. To celebrate the things the team did well and to learn from its mistakes.

Time

1 hour

Materials

Flip chart paper, index cards or sticky notes, marking pens

Purpose/Objectives

- To debrief the experiences and efforts of the team together

- To learn from their missteps

- To celebrate the things they did well

Grouping

All team members

Warm-up

Explain that the team is dissolving and that we want to take time to learn from our experiences as a team. We want to celebrate those areas where we did well and to learn from the activities or products that could have been better.

Aerobics

1. Label two flip charts, one "Prouds" and one "Regrets."

2. Ask team members to write on index cards or sticky notes behaviors, activities, products, and anything they are proud the team accomplished.

3. Write only one idea on each card or note. Make them large enough to read from a distance.

4. Post the cards or notes under each heading on the flip charts.

5. Everyone reads the posted notes.

6. Ask if there are questions or need for clarification.

7. Look for the main ideas and themes.

8. Summarize on the flip charts the prouds and the regrets.

9. File in the team's archives.

Cooldown

Go around the room and ask each person to give one statement that reflects the accomplishments of the team.

Adapted from ideas of ASQ Press reviewers

Accountability

How Did We Do?

Workout Plan

When to use
When the team is dissolving and members want to revisit their experiences and their outputs.

Time
1 hour

Materials
How Did We Do? Worksheet
Flip chart and markers

Purpose/Objectives

- To debrief the project, team effort, or team products

- To provide information to others who may need to know about the team's work

- To provide a common understanding of the team's work

Grouping
All team members

Warm-up
Distribute the How Did We Do? Worksheet to each member before the meeting. Explain that the purpose of the meeting is to discuss

the work of the team, what we did well, and where we can improve in future efforts.

Aerobics

1. Ask members, round robin, to discuss each question on the worksheet in order.

2. Write the main points on the flip chart.

3. Decide which points should be recorded and placed in the archives of the team's project.

Cooldown

Ask each team member to give a single sincere statement about how it's been for him to work on this team.

HOW DID WE DO? WORKSHEET

Dear Team Members,

At our meeting _____, we will plan to discuss our team's performance prior to the dissolution of our team. These topics will provide insight for each of us to use in our future team situations and provide documentation regarding our current team efforts.

Take a few minutes to consider the following questions. Jot down your notes and bring them to the meeting.

Think about the outcomes of our efforts, the processes we used, how we worked together.

1. What I liked about this team and would want to have again in working with future teams.

2. What I would change or adjust in a future team situation.

G. Celebrations

Celebrations were very important to team leaders. Here are some examples of how teams have celebrated their achievements and milestones. (Don't wait until the end of the project.) Be imaginative, and design a celebration appropriate to your situation and locale!

> We have a fun Friday each month. We always do something different. Some examples are:
> - Went to Star Wars.
> - Ate lunch on a sunny deck and paddled around in paddle boats on a lake
> - We went fishing
> - Went to an Irish Pub.
>
> *Bill Gardner, Advanced Micro Devices*

We climbed Mt. Whitney.

Gary Dyer,
Southwestern
Farm Credit

We use a certificate with thanks from the company to them and boss and bosses' boss.

Too many people to cite

We get together and horse around. Play practical jokes. We do the ropes course, play games like Trivial Pursuit, celebrate with cookouts and family get togethers.

Nick Rakos,
TU Electric

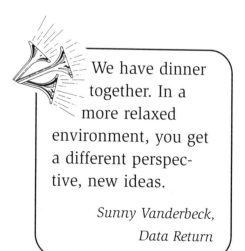

We have dinner together. In a more relaxed environment, you get a different perspective, new ideas.

Sunny Vanderbeck,
Data Return

Sometimes we (with spouses) play on a soccer team, do Red Cross work, play on a cricket team, bring in customers to see the plant and serve tea and cakes (like family), or take trips to see product installation in pipe organs.

Duncan Crundwell, Solid State Logic

Celebrations are very important. We get together and go out to relax. We talk about our accomplishments and celebrate each other usually at a waterfront cafe. It's important to celebrate, but we try to balance work time and personal time.

Joan Gotti, Chase Manhattan

Celebrations are particular to the team. We went to a movie filmed at the office next door.

Name withheld upon request

We declared our own casual days. Then we declared a casual day for the whole company in recognition of hitting a milestone.

Bob Miller, Gates Rubber Company

No one had been bowling, but we are all competitive. We drew names out of a hat after the game to see who was on each team; therefore, we cheered for everyone all through the games because we didn't know who was on our team.

Bill Gardner, Advanced Micro Devices

We use noisemakers and horns and march around. We engage support staff in victories so they see line of sight from their work to victory, to laws passing.

Name withheld upon request

Families are important with some teams.

1. Attend children's affairs at school

2. Gifts to families and children

3. Family get togethers

4. Cookouts

Too many people to cite

Epilogue

Dear Reader,

My goal for this book was to give you some insights from the field, from other team leaders like yourself, plus some observations of my own. This book can serve as a framework on which you can arrange your own thoughts and activities. Use the exercises like a menu and choose the ones that suit your needs.

Often teams are isolated, with no one to talk to or to provide encouragement. Sometimes they are hidden in staid hierarchical organizations. Perhaps the best thing this book can do for you is to provide reinforcement of the good things you're already doing.

The book is finished, but a team's fitness, like our own mental and physical fitness, is never finished. Because we are all human and you and your team are human beings, we are all "works in progress." Team fitness is a continuous process. It can also be an exhilarating one where you can see personal growth in other members and outcomes that surpass your expectations.

As we said before, have patience, be real, keep the faith.

All the best wishes for the success of your team.

Jane E. Henry

Bibliography

Adams, J. L. *Conceptual Blockbusting: A Guide to Better Ideas.* Reading, MA: Addison-Wesley, 1974, pp. 24–33.

ASQC. *Quality Management Journal,* Special Teams Issue, 4, no. 2 (1997).

Berry, L. L., Bennett, D. R., & Brown, C. W. *Service Quality: A Profit Strategy for Financial Institutions.* Homewood, IL: Dow Jones-Irwin, 1989.

Blanchard, K., Carew, D., & Parisi-Carew, E. *One Minute Manager Builds High Performing Teams.* New York: William Morrow, 1990.

Bridges, W. *Managing Transitions: Making the Most of Change.* Reading, MA: Addison-Wesley, 1991.

Collins, J. L., & Porras, J. I., *Built to Last: Successful Habits of Visionary Companies.* New York: HarperCollins, 1994.

DeBono, E. *Six Thinking Hats.* Boston: Little, Brown, 1985.

Hartzler, M., & Henry, J. E. *Team Fitness: A How-to Manual for Building a Winning Work Team.* Milwaukee, WI: ASQC Quality Press, 1994.

Henry, J. E., & Hartzler, M. *Tools for Virtual Teams: A Team Fitness Companion.* Milwaukee, WI: ASQC Quality Press, 1998.

IMST. *Master Clips: Thumbnail Catalog.* San Rafael, CA: IMST, 1995.

Katzenbach, J.R., & Smith, D.K. *The Wisdom of Teams.* Boston: Harvard Business School Press, 1993.

Krakauer, J. *Into Thin Air: A Personal Account of the Mt. Everest Disaster.* New York: Villard Books, 1997.

Uchida, R. *Kathmandu to Everest.* Huddersfield, England: Springfield Books, 1991.

Index

A

Accountability, in inititaion
  of team, 47
Agreements, of team, 105–6
Assessments, 122–23

B

Books
  reading of, 144–46
  use of, 27–28
Buy-in of decisions, with
  teamwork, 4–5

C

Celebrations, 177–81
Charrette, 62–64
Charter, 56–61
  summary sheet, 60–61
  workout plan, 56–57
  worksheet for, 58–59

Clean up task, of leader,
  37–38
Client service survey, example, 120–21
Climate, of workplace, enjoyability of, with teams,
  5–6
Communication
  improvement in, with
    teamwork, 4–5
  networks, 140–43
  exercise, 143
Complacency, of team, 113
Completion of project,
  163–75
  accomplishments, 167–68
    objectives, 167
    workout plan, 167–68
  method of, 164–65
  peer recognition poster,
    169–70
    workout plan, 169–70

performance overview,
  173–75
  workout plan, 173–74
  worksheet for, 175
regrets, 171–72
Complexity of tasks, need for
  team with, 2
Consultant, alien, exercise,
  152–53
Continuous improvement, of
  team, 28
Creativity, stimulation of,
  with teamwork, 3–4
Cross-training, of teams,
  109–10
Customer
  focus
    interviews, 51–53
    worksheet for, 54–55
  voice of, 117–21

D

Debriefing, 137–39
  worksheet for, 139
Decision analysis, weighted,
    126–28
  worksheet for, 128
Decisions
  improvement in, with
      teamwork, 2–3
  ownership of, with team-
      work, 4–5
Dissolution of team, 28,
    163–75. *See* Ending of
    team
Diversity, in team, 32

E

Ending of team, 163–75
  accomplishments, 167–68
    objectives, 167
    workout plan, 167–68
  method of, 164–65
  peer recognition poster,
      169–70
    workout plan, 169–70
  performance overview,
      173–75
    workout plan, 173–74
    worksheet for, 175
  regrets, 171–72
Everest, assault on, exercise,
    157–62
  worksheet for, 162

F

Feedback, 133–36
  peer performance review,
      136
  of teams, 110–11
Fitness of team, model, 9–26,
    10
  accountability, *19*, 19, 22
    defined, 19
    implementation plan-
        ning, defined, 22

operating agreements,
    defined, 22
  project planning,
    defined, 22
beliefs, defined, 19
charter, defined, 13
client interview questions,
    12
core values-example, 23
customer focus, 10, *11*
  goals, 13
direction, 13–16, *14*
  mission statement, 14
    example, 15
  mission, defined, 13
  objectives, 13
  reliability management,
      24–25
  understanding, *17*, 17–19
    defined, 17
  values, defined, 19
  vision, defined, 13
Focus, customer
  interviews, 51–55
  worksheet for, 54–55
Frustrations, of teams, 111–16

G

Goals, in inititaion of team,
    46–47

H

Huddle, team in, 147–48

I

Implementation planning,
    96–99
  confidentiality, 97
  of team, tentative, 48
  workout plan, 96–97
  worksheet for, 98
  critique of, 99
Improvement, continuous,
    28, 107–62
  alien consultant exercise,
      152–53

assault on Everest exercise,
    157–62
  worksheet for, 162
assessment, 122–23
book, reading of, 144–46
client service survey,
    example, 120–21
communication networks,
    140–43
  exercise, 143
cross-training, 109–10
customer, voice of, 117–21
debriefing, 137–39
  worksheet for, 139
feedback, 110–11, 133–36
  peer performance
      review, 136
frustrations, 111–16
huddle, 147–48
overview, 107
paradigm, development of,
    129–32
problem, worksheet for,
    131
strategic planning, 122–23
training, 108–9
vision, creation of, 124–25
weighted decision analysis,
    126–28
  worksheet for, 128
Innovation, stimulation of,
    with teamwork, 3–4
Interview, selection, 81–83
  workout plan, 81–82
  worksheet for, 83
Interviews, customer focus,
    51–55
Introduction, of team mem-
    bers, 84–88
  interview questions, 86
  workout plan, 84–86
  worksheet for, 87–88

L

Leader, role of, 31–40
  clean up task, 37–38

diversity, 32
formation of team, 32
new leader, 36–38
new team, selection of, 32–34
success in, 6–7

M
Map for team, 65–69
  example, 69
  workout plan, 65–67
  worksheet for, 68
Meetings rules, 100–104
  agenda, example, 104
  celebrations, 48–49
  mission for team, 46
  objectives, 46–47
  recognition, 48–49
  rewards, 48–49
  rules, 100–104
  workout plan, 100–1, 105–6
  worksheet for, 102–3
Mission statement of team, 70–73
  workout plan, 70–72
  worksheet for, 73
Model, team fitness, 9–26, *10*
  accountability, *19,* 19–20
    implementation planning, defined, 22
    operating agreements, defined, 22
    project planning, defined, 22
  charter, defined, 13
  client interview questions, 12
  core values-example, 23
  customer focus, 10, *11*
    goals, 13
    direction, 13–16, *14*
    accountability, defined, 19
    beliefs, defined, 19
    defined, 10

mission statement, 14
  example, 15
  understanding, defined, 17
  values, defined, 19
mission, defined, 13
objectives, 13
reliability management, 24–25
understanding, *17,* 17–19
vision, defined, 13

N
Need for teams, 1–7
Networks, for communication, 140–43
  exercise, 143
New leader, 36–37
New team
  leader of, 32–34
  selection of, 32–34

O
Operating agreements, of team, 47–49
Opportunity for success, with teams, 5–6
Ownership of decisions, with teamwork, 4–5

P
Paradigm, development of, 129–32
Peer performance review, for feedback, 136
Performance review, for feedback, 136
Picture, creating vision with, 124–25
Planning
  implementation, 96–99
    confidentiality, 97
    workout plan, 96–97
    worksheet for, 98
      critique of, 99

strategic, 122–23
Principles of team, 89–92
  accountability, 93–94
  example, 92
  workout plan, 89–90
  worksheet for, 91
Problems, worksheet for for, 131
Product quality, 118

Q
Quality, of product, 118

R
Rationale for teams, 1–7
Reading of books, 144–46
Results, improvement in, with teamwork, 2–3
Review, of performance, for feedback, 136
Rewards, in inititaion of team, 48–49
Road map for team, 65–69
  example, 69
  workout plan, 65–67
  worksheet for, 68
Role of leader, 31–40
  clean up task, 37–39
  diversity, 32
  formation of team, 32
  new leader, 36–37
  new team, selection of, 32–35
Rules, for meetings, 100–104
  agenda, example, 104
  celebrations, 48–49
  mission for team, 46
  objectives, 46–47
  recognition, 48–49
  rewards, 48–49
  rules, 100–4
  workout plan, 100–1, 105–6
  worksheet for, 102–3

S

Selection interview, 81–83
  workout plan, 81–82
  worksheet for, 83
Selection of new team, 32–34
Service, to client, survey,
    example, 120–21
Start-up of team
  accountability, 46
  agreements, of team,
      105–6
  basic principles, 89–92
    accountability, 93–94
    example, 95
    workout plan, 89–90
    worksheet for, 91
  charrette, 62–64
  charter, 56–61
    summary sheet, 60–61
    workout plan, 56–57
    worksheet for, 58–59
  customer focus, 95
    interviews, 51–55
    worksheet for, 54–55
  goals, 46–47
  implementation planning,
      96–99
    confidentiality, 97
    workout plan, 96–97
    worksheet for, 98
    critique of, 99
  introduction of members,
      84–85
    interview questions, 86
    workout plan, 84–85
    worksheet for, 87–88
  meetings rules, 100–104
    agenda, example, 104
  celebrations, 48–49
  mission for team, 46
  objectives, 46–47
  recognition, 48–49
  rewards, 48–49
  rules, 100–104

  workout plan, 100–101,
      105–6
    worksheet for, 102–3
  mission statement, 70–73
    workout plan, 70–72
    worksheet for, 73
  operating agreements,
      47–48
  rewards, 48–49
  road map, 65–69
    example, 69
    workout plan, 65–67
    worksheet for, 68
  selection interview, 81–83
    workout plan, 81–82
    worksheet for, 83
  tentative implementation
      plan, 48
  transition, 74–76
  values, 93–95
    start-up—example, 95
    workout plan, 93–94
  vision, 46, 77–79
    pictures, creating vision
        with, 124–25
    words, creating vision
        with, 77
    workout plan, 77–79
  workout plan, 51–53
    aerobics, 52–53
    cooldown, 53
    grouping, 52
    materials, 51
    purpose, 51
    time, 51
    warm-up, 52
Statement, of mission of
    team, 70–72
  workout plan, 70–72
  worksheet for, 73
Strategic planning, 122–23
Success, opportunity for,
    with teams, 5–6
Successful leaders, of teams,
    6–7

Summary sheet, charter,
    60–61

T

Tasks, complexity of, need
    for team with, 2
Team values, and agree-
    ments, 105–6
Tentative implementation
    plan, of team, 48
Training, of teams, 108–9
Transition, in team, 74–76

V

Values of team, 93–95
  start-up-example, 95
  workout plan, 93–94
Vision of team, 77–79
  creation of, 124–25
  pictures, creating vision
      with, 124–25
  in team initiation, 45
  words, creating vision
      with, 77
  workout plan, 77–79
  worksheet, 80

W

Weighted decision analysis,
    126–28
  worksheet for, 128
Winding-up of team, 163–75
  accomplishments, 167–68
    objectives, 167
    workout plan, 167–68
  method of, 164–65
  peer recognition poster,
      169–70
    workout plan, 169–70
  performance overview,
      173–75
    workout plan, 173–74
    worksheet for, 175
  regrets, 171–72
Work climate, enjoyability of,
    with teams, 5–6

Comments and Areas for Improvement:
Lessons From Team Leaders

Please give us your comments, feedback, and suggestions for making this book more useful. We believe in the importance of continuous improvement and in meeting your needs. Your comments will help determine what improvements can be made in all ASQ Quality Press books.

Please share your opinion by circling the number below:

Ratings of the book	Needs Work		Satisfactory		Excellent	Comments
Structure, flow, and logic	1	2	3	4	5	
Content, ideas, and information	1	2	3	4	5	
Style, clarity, ease of reading	1	2	3	4	5	
Held my interest	1	2	3	4	5	
Met my overall expectations	1	2	3	4	5	

I read the book because:

The best part of the book was:

The least satisfactory part of the book was:

Other suggestions for improvement:

General comments:

Name/Address: (optional)

Thank you for your feedback. If you do not have access to a fax machine, please mail this form to:
ASQ Quality Press, 611 East Wisconsin Avenue, P.O. Box 3005, Milwaukee, WI 53201-3005   Phone: 414-272-8575